Enc

This book takes seriously the responsibility for Christians to relevantly participate in the Great Commission and in the challenging issues facing our world. In particular, the authors have done a great job in detailing the responsibility to comprehensively support our mission personnel who are serving Christ in new ways and in difficult settings. Through many practical examples and personal experiences, the Trinity MC Team points the way forward for other churches to consider as they further develop their own member care programs—to know their mission personnel well (close relationships) and to care for their mission personnel well (competent services) (Proverbs 27: 23-24). This book builds upon the many helpful church-related materials in the member care literature by adding a wealth of specific ideas, suggestions, and tools for guidance. The member care field will be stronger because of this instructive book, especially as the field continues to branch out into new areas of service (e.g., supporting the diversity of people who are working across cultures, generations, issues, sectors, etc.). We are grateful for the terrific team effort modeled by its authors and for their hands-on commitment to the well-being and effectiveness of mission personnel working throughout our very needy world.

Dr. Kelly O'Donnell and
Dr. Michèle Lewis O'Donnell
Consulting Psychologists, Member Care Associates, Inc.

Mind the Gaps is a vibrant, timely, and relevant book that will move a standard Mission Committee that oversees mission funds and arranges occasional Mission Conferences to an involved and energetic Missionary Care team... I know of no other book like it. This volume will be incredibly useful to any church that wants to become more missional, and wants to be energetically and compassionately involved in the workers they deploy.

Laura Mae Gardner
Wycliffe

Trinity Church, under the leadership of Mission Pastor David Wilson, has undertaken a most thoughtful and comprehensive study of the multiple facets of missionary care. Every one is germane to the well-being of a church's cross-cultural outreach ministry. The whole team is to be commended. However, of greater importance is that you, the reader, "Get on Board" and prayerfully apply these principles to your individual fellowship.

Neal Pirolo
Director, Emmaus Road International
Author, *Serving as Senders Today*
www.eri.org

Obedience to God's call draws missionaries into many profoundly new, potentially disorienting, and sometimes traumatic and lonely experiences. Loving, grace-filled relationships with the supportive community of their sending church provides resilience that is essential for their growth and their ministries to flourish. Sending churches have a unique opportunity to uphold these disciples through relationships that emphasize personal caring while the missionaries minister to others. This outstanding book imparts a wealth of mission specific knowledge in a practical and accessible manner written by people who clearly know and have experienced the mission field themselves.

Charlie Schaefer
Charles A. Schaefer, Ph.D., Inc.
Co-Author, *Trauma & Resilience: Effectively Supporting Those Who Serve God*
Mental Health and Missions Conference
www.CharlieSchaefer.com

I believe this book will be a tremendous addition to the existing literature on missionary care from the church side of the equation. I trust and pray that it will have a huge impact on those who choose to read and implement your suggestions. I will probably order a case myself when they become available! May God continue to guide you in the process of publishing it.

I read dozens of books every year on the topic of missionary care; I have never read anything like this. *Mind the Gaps* is a much-needed and long-overdue addition to the discussion of how to practically care for the harvest workers we send out. This book is full of good information, but more importantly, it has the potential to act as a catalyst for expanding the conversation. Read it, then join the conversation.

Dave Lewis
President, Paracletos, Inc.
Equipping the church to care for the harvest force
www.paracletos.org

"They have an excellent grasp of what missionaries really face!"

Dave & Pris Reimer
Avant Ministries

Fulfilling the great commission is too great a task to accomplish alone. We all need to be engaged in the task, whether it is serving on the front lines, or providing a support network for those who do. Helpful, effective partnerships between church and missionary involve more than writing checks and offering occasional prayers. *Mind the Gaps* identifies some of the unique needs of cross-cultural workers and gives encouragement and practical suggestions for coming alongside as caring, supportive partners in ministry.

Lois McMartin
Director of Member Care
Evangelical Free Church of America
ReachGlobal

Many churches express a desire to provide better care for their missionaries. *Mind the Gaps* presents practical, realistic ways a church can do this. It is easy to read, easy to learn from, and covers areas which most churches do not even think about. This book fills a gap. I recommend it to every missionary care team.

Dr. Debbie Hawker
Executive Committee member,
Global Member Care Network
www.resilientexpat.co.uk

There is a growing awareness in the North American evangelical church of the importance of global missionary care. For years the church has come alongside missionaries to provide prayer and financial support...but how wonderful to see the church embracing the Biblical mandate to care also for the spiritual and emotional needs of those they send out. *Mind the Gaps* is filled with practical ideas to help the church engage with global missions by providing heart care to their mission teams. This is a "must read" for any church that wants to fully understand their God given call to shepherd their workers."

Perry Bradford
Executive Director
Barnabas International

It is a delight to endorse this book. This is such an important subject, but one that has been long overlooked. I believe that most churches leave the care of their missionaries to the agencies. In my opinion this is a great mistake. The sending church has a unique responsibility and relationship to its missionary. This very practical, 'how-to' book is a must read for anyone in the church who has an interest in providing care for their church's missionaries.

David Harthan
Counseling Associate
TEAM (The Evangelical Alliance Mission)

Mind the Gaps is a much needed resource in which the rise of church based teams is becoming a significant force. There is a healthy respect for the "triad of care" (agencies, churches and individuals) reflected in these pages and an honest look at the dilemmas that occur when agencies and churches seek to care for overseas workers. This is a book that I would want my agency and church to read as they seek to care for my personal needs as an international worker.

Colleen Wong
Barnabas International
co-author of *Tender Care*

We view the church as a strategic partner in sending out missionaries from our organization to wherever in the world God has led them to serve. While some churches have well developed missionary care structures, there are many which are unaware of how to care for their people. I am grateful this book can now be a resource to share with our appointees and their sending churches. Within these pages are both principles and practical tools to be adopted by mission committees of varying sizes. Well done!

Faith De La Cour
Director of Member Care
SIM USA

As a former cross-cultural worker who once stood broken and in need of care, I enthusiastically endorse this book. I am deeply burdened to mobilize the Church, as the missionary sending body, to engage in compassionate care of its kingdom workers. This will most certainly be required reading for our ministry students in our college. My prayer is for this book to gain a wide readership and broad influence.

Greg Mann
Director of Missions
Trinity Baptist Church/Trinity Baptist College
Jacksonville, Florida

At last, a missionary care manual written *for* sending churches *by* a sending church. This is a hands-on, how-to book for church leaders who want to know how to start, or start over, in caring for missionaries from beginning to end. Here you will learn how to choose a sending team from within the church, how to select a mission agency, how to prepare your missionaries, how to let them feel your love, how to heal the brokenhearted, how to help them persevere, and how to welcome them home. Church leaders who want to know that the care of missionary families and singles is going to be complex and demanding, will want to read this book. It will make a dream become a reality; it will turn your "What if?" into "What is."

Bob Blincoe, Ph.D.
US Director
Frontiers

A brilliant treasure chest of time-tested collective wisdom! This book is must read for any Church already engaged in, or interested in beginning the great privilege of caring for missionaries.

Brian Mount
Vice President Global Talent
Operation Mobilization, USA

What an excellent resource this is! I found that it rang true with my experience with a missionary's need for care from their sending churches. I particularly liked that the book is very practical. While providing appropriate background they did not make theory the main point of the book. Their examples show other churches how to do it without insisting that their 'method' is the only way. They outline the steps a church can take in each area to develop their own member care plan. The questions at the end of each chapter make this a workbook that can be easily followed. The book is so comprehensive that even a church, which is already doing a good job, will pick up ways to enhance what they are already doing. This book is all-inclusive, in that it does not just deal with crisis situations. It covers needs that all missionaries have starting from their first interest in missions through their retirement. Finally, I like the emphasis on the church and agency serving together as partners in missionary care. Both are responsible for providing care for missionaries. As they say, there are gaps and will always be gaps in care. If both agency and church "mind the gap" we will promote the well-being, resilience, and sustainability of missionaries who are giving their lives for the sake of the gospel. Thank you for your labor of love in writing this book. It is needed and will be widely used.

Steven G. Edlin, MA LCPC MFT
Member Care Director
T.E.A.M

I'm celebrating the publication of this book! One of the most important areas of need and potential in missions today involves the ongoing role of the sending church in providing for the health and effectiveness of its missionaries. All too often this topic has become a source of confusion and disappointment between the missionary, sending church and agency. *Mind the Gaps* is a wonderfully practical tool, full of experience and real-life case studies, that will help dispel the mystery and pave the way to greater fruitfulness. I hope every church missions team will study these chapters and take advantage of the supplemental resources at www.MindTheGaps.org.

Steve Richardson
President
Pioneers-USA

I wholeheartedly recommend *Mind the Gaps* for anyone who cares about missions and missionaries. This book in itself fills a gap in the missionary care world by giving churches a practical, full-orbed model for keeping missionaries healthy and on the field. It is written by a team of people who speak from a wealth of experience in caring for missionaries from a local church perspective. They are refreshingly honest about their struggles as they worked to put together a team and process to effectively care for the people in ministry that they support as a church. From my own interactions with this team, I know that they do not only talk about working together with mission agencies to care for missionaries. They practice what they preach."

J. Timothy Smith, LPC
Member Care
Prepare/Enrich Certified Counselor
Greater Europe Mission

As someone who has been invested in the care of missionaries as part of a mission agency, I am so thankful for a resource like *Mind the Gaps*. A strong partnership between the church, the missionary, and the agency are key to successful long-term ministry, particularly during hard times. *Mind the Gaps* provides a clear plan for ways that we can support one another in our areas of strength, allowing us to serve together more fully as the body of Christ.

Jennifer Holloran, SPHR
Chief Human Resources Officer
Wycliffe Bible Translators

MIND THE GAPS

ENGAGING THE CHURCH IN MISSIONARY CARE

Additional authors:
Linda Parker
William G. Britt, III
Susanne Hood
William and Betty Jane Born

Unless otherwise noted, all scripture references are from the English Standard Version
Unless otherwise noted, all personal stories are taken from agencies, churches and missionaries worldwide. Names and places have been changed to ensure confidentiality.

Published By: Mind the Gaps
Cover Design: Laura Drew
Typesetting: Michelle VanGeest

ISBN 978-0-578-16053-5

Library of Congress Control No. 2015905944

Printed in the United States of America

Acknowledgements

Collaborating to write a book with six authors could provide the subject matter for an additional book. For the last three years, we have travelled together to some of the most remote places on earth. We spent many hours together in the upper room of the church building, in each others homes, and a few weekend retreats in a mountain cabin just so that we could do peer reviews of partially completed chapters. We attended seminars, conferences, and forums to learn from the best of the best. We read books on Member Care and debated issues related to best practices. We also practiced our insights on a regular basis with our own missionaries. Sometimes we walked away in agreement and other times we just walked away… always with love, admiration and respect for the person with a differing point of view.

We owe an enormous debt to the member care community who organize the Global Member Care Network through the World Evangelical Alliance. After attending the conference in 2012 in Chiang Mai, Thailand, our team went to Tioman Island off the coast of Malaysia for debriefing, and that is where we made the decision to write this book. Thanks to Harry Hoffmann, Debbie Hawker, Brent Lindquist and all the others who serve so tirelessly to inform and equip providers as they care for missionaries.

We have thoroughly enjoyed being invited to attend church partnership events with some of our partner agencies. God is truly drawing the church and the agency together in very strategic ways. Our team has been honored to attend many gatherings where churches and agencies get together and dialogue about how we can partner together. Specifically, we wish to recognize Frontiers, Pioneers, OM, SIM and TEAM for hosting us at your headquarters. Thanks for the hospitality and the vision to let the church be intimately involved in the work of the Kingdom with you.

Wisdom in counseling is often summed up in this phrase: "Know when to refer." That is why we love our partners in the ministry who do specialized care services like Barnabas International, Link Care, Missionary Training International (MTI) and the Center for Intercultural Training (CIT). Most of our work as caregivers can be managed between the church and the agency, but there are times, when our people need special attention, and we thank God for those with extraordinary talents in the arts of training, equipping, healing and restoration.

Mind the Gaps provides a distinct contribution to existing member care literature because it is collaboratively written by an experienced and practicing missionary care team from a local church. Though this is written from the perspective of a local church, it stands on the shoulders of a much larger body of literature. A quick glance at author names on my bookshelf includes multiple volumes by O'Donnell, Schaefer, Pirolo and Powell. A special thanks to the authors of Tender Care for meeting with us and helping us collaborate as authors. Due to the places where you work, we cannot publish your identity, but you know who you are. We also wish to give special thanks to Laura Mae Gardner for your encouragement, your love and gentle guidance as we walked this path together. You are a blessing!

Every author knows the value of editors. This was especially true for us as we sought to write a book from multiple perspectives and multiple writing styles. You took our words and framed them so that they make sense, yet you allowed us to 'keep our voices' within the text. Thanks Sandee Foster, Lorene Wilson and Tracy Calzaretta for reading, commenting, questioning, editing, correcting and loving us along this journey. Also, thanks to Becky Dau and Beth Tabor for your unique contribution to this work.

The Lord has blessed Trinity Church with this assembly of skilled and passionate people so that they could write this book to be a blessing to other churches and individuals who want to serve their oversees workers. He has uniquely gifted each and every local church with a variety of resources, which can be mobilized to minister overseas. Missionaries need proactive spiritual, emotional, practical and professional care, rather than just reactive responses to problems. That is why the authors of *Mind the Gaps* believe that the local church should have a major and strategic role to play in helping the missionaries it sends to thrive in the place where God sends them.

Our final and primary acknowledgment goes out to our very own beloved Trinity Church missionary family with a deep and abiding appreciation. We pray that churches everywhere will discover and adopt a system of proactive care, which will ensure lasting engagement of both the church and the agency into the lives of missionary families scattered across the globe. This book was written for you and now we dedicate it to you. May the Lord help us as we *Mind the Gaps* of care together.

MIND THE GAPS

ENGAGING THE CHURCH IN MISSIONARY CARE

Foreword

The Mind the Gaps team has written *Mind the Gaps*, a vibrant, timely, and relevant book that will move a staid Mission Committee that arranges occasional Mission Conferences to an involved and energetic Missionary Care Team.

Some of the uniquenesses of this book are the scope of the plan and the practical nature of the contributions. These authors have done their home work. Realizing that considerable effort must go into the groundwork of such a team, they begin with choice of people to be on their Care Team, establishing a Philosophy of Ministry, and Core Values, and compatibility of their efforts with the strategic focus of the church. Each of these basic topics is presented in the form of policies, and a copy of the policy is included.

A key section has to do with the prospective worker—what are the predictors of missionary success and how can the Care Team do its part in the selection process? The book then launches into relationships, meeting of needs and managing transitions.

They deal head on with the delicate issue of confidentiality.

A major section in the book covers relationships—Care Team to missionaries, missionaries to the congregation, and Care Team with the sending agency. The authors serve as brokers to involve the whole congregation with the missionaries as well as to deal respectfully with the agency.

The authors do not sidestep difficult issues, such as on-field conflict, insubordination or lack of productivity of the worker or lack of communication, but they deal with these challenges in a courageous and compassionate way.

I was blessed by my careful reading of the book. I know of no other book like it. This volume will be incredibly useful to any church that wants to become more missional, and wants to be energetically and compassionately involved in the workers they deploy. If the suggestions given by the authors are followed, it will revitalize the church and the congregation!

Laura Mae Gardner
Wycliffe and the Summer Institute of Linguistics
International Personnel Consultant and Trainer

Introduction

David Wilson

In 1968 the London Transportation System coined the term "Mind the Gap" to warn people of the danger of falling from the subway platform onto the tracks as they wait for, or step onto, the train. The phrase caught on and is now used to caution people at subway stations around the world from New York to Japan. Even with warning signs and safety precautions in place, accidents still happen and call for human intervention. One of the most amazing interventions was on January 2, 2007, when New York subway hero Wesley Autrey made a split second decision to throw his body over Cameron Hollopeter, a young man who had a seizure and fell off the subway platform into the path of an oncoming train. The train roared over them close enough to leave grease on Autrey's cap! *Extraordinary* was the country's reaction to his heroic act and people from near and far showered him with gifts, including $10,000 from Donald Trump. "I don't feel like I did something spectacular," he said afterward, "I just saw someone who needed help. I did what I felt was right." Going deeper into this story, however reveals something truly extraordinary. Autrey, having worked in confined spaces as a construction worker was in a unique position to judge that there was enough room under the train for Hallopeter and himself. Autrey, an ordinary person, stepped in to meet a need that probably only he could have had the courage and insight to fill at that moment, even if the professional rescue workers were present. Fortunately for Hollopeter, Autrey was there to "mind the gap" for him.

When it comes to caring for missionaries, the church should see itself in the same role in which Autrey found himself. We send our missionaries out under the care of competent professionals (the mission agency) many of which have infrastructure in place to care for the needs of our people, and for the most part, they do very well. But the church is uniquely equipped to minister to its missionaries, especially when it sees gaps in care that the agencies, for whatever reason, do not or cannot provide.

Thanks to the recent development and expansion of mission agencies, the gospel is being proclaimed at an unprecedented rate. However, most agencies today will tell you that they are understaffed and many are overwhelmed with the enormous needs of their members. The numbers of missionaries sent out to remote fields are at an all-time high, and the complexity of challenges which they face is immense.

Gaps in giving care are not just a result of understaffing, but these gaps are also apparent in the practices from one agency to another. Some agencies have well developed member care departments while others have not. There may be a deficit in adequate supervision, oversight, accountability, contingency plans and strategic focus planning that can aid missionaries in achieving kingdom objectives. The church should step forward with determination and respond to the call of caring *proactively* for missionaries, not just *reactively* when a need arises. *Mind the Gaps* is intended to empower churches, to complement and enhance the efforts of the member care department of agencies, and to reduce the attrition rate of missionaries who are sent out to the field.

Some would argue that parachurch organizations (such as the mission agency) exist today as a direct result of the inactivity of the church. That is certainly not the opinion of this writer. As the late Dr. Ralph Winter believed, "our efforts today in any part of the world will be most effective only if both of these two structures [the church and agencies] are fully and properly involved and supportive of each other." *(Dr. Ralph Winter—The Two Structures of God's Redemptive Mission, http://resources.campusforchrist.org/images/4/48/The_Parachurch.pdf)* Mission agencies are fulfilling a very strategic role within the kingdom of God. However, the Church is the body of Christ which has been mandated with God's plan of redemption for the nations. Therefore, it would be negligent to simply delegate or outsource the responsibility of missionary care completely to agencies.

The church should have a major and strategic role to play in helping the missionaries it sends to thrive in the place where God sends them. We invested in them often from birth, nurtured them for service unto the Lord, instilled in them the desire to minister in other cultures, prayed with them and raised funds to put them on the field. We have relationships of trust already in place which enable us to be a great encouragement to them. We also have an abundance of people with skills, gifts and abilities to serve them through relationships.

That is what this book is about. We hope to show the ways in which the local church is uniquely equipped to minister to the missionaries it sends and to mind the gaps of needs which are not always met by agencies. In preparation for writing this book, our team interviewed member care professionals within agencies and from missionary training and retreat centers. We participated in conferences, symposia and seminars. We consumed numerous books on the topic and also have been fully engaged in the practice of missionary care as a team. Much of what we found is a lack of specific focus in helping to develop and nurture a church-based missionary care team. That is why we have collaborated to write this book together as a team of caring and committed Christ followers with a passion for helping missionaries remain on the field and be productive catalysts for the expansion of God's kingdom.

As you read Part One, we hope you will put together a team of volunteers, if you don't already have one, which will identify these gaps of care for your particular missionaries, and develop strategies unique to how God has equipped your church to minister. In Part Two, we look at predictors of missionary success as well as aligning the missionaries you send with the strategic focus of your church. Though vetting missionaries is not necessarily a part of missionary care, we included a section on how to wisely choose the people you send, because most of us in missionary care have seen the heartache of people who should never have been sent. In Part Three, we will look at how you can capitalize on the relationships in your church to encourage and help sustain your missionaries, as well as how to develop collaborative relationships with the mission agencies to coordinate care. In Part Four, we'll help you understand the unique needs of missionaries, the effect of mission life on their emotional and spiritual well-being and how to utilize resources in your church to minister practically to them to enhance their effectiveness on the field. And, in Part Five, we will take a look at transitions such as furlough, home assignment, changes in assignment, and end of career.

By minding the gaps in missionary care, the church can create a system of proactive care which will ensure lasting engagement of both the local church and the agency into the lives of our precious and beloved missionaries. We have collaborated to write this book from a variety of perspectives, and our hope is that it will be only the first stage in this process for you. One of the subtitles that we considered was, "Our Journey Thus Far," meaning that we are not writing this because we have it all figured out. We are on a journey with many unscheduled stops, complex transfers and signs which read "Under Construction." In many ways this is a venture in learning for us, so that we can process what we have accomplished and then apply lessons learned for future success.

After the bombing raid on Pearl Harbor, Japanese Admiral Yamamoto said, "I fear all we have done is to awaken a sleeping giant." Throughout the centuries, the Church has been very effective in many ways, "a giant" for the gospel. Schools and hospitals have been built, poverty and crime issues have been addressed, frameworks of justice and morality have influenced legal systems and of course the gospel of Jesus Christ is being proclaimed to all nations. For a variety of reasons, when it comes to missionary care, the church could be perceived as a sleeping giant. Many mission agencies have perfected the ministry of member care over the years and they may feel threatened by churches that are "interfering." Churches are often complacent and comfortable with just sending a check as their sole means of support for missionaries. However, we believe that God is calling the Church to rise up and be an answer to prayer for missionaries who are serving the world on our behalf. Through humble and genuine partnership with the agencies, we can foster effective ministries through missionaries who stay on the field longer. Waking a giant is risky business, and to wake this sleeping giant is our goal in this book.

May the words from our keyboard and the meditation from our collaboration be pleasing and acceptable in His sight. As we all seek to serve the Lord together, we present to you—*Mind the Gaps!*

PART ONE

All Aboard

Getting Started

Chapter 1

People For Your Team

Linda Parker

> "We must demystify missionary care from the preconception that this ministry is only for professional mental health providers or seminary-trained pastors. It is not our competence but our character that is most essential in this work—humility, authenticity and the fragrance of having had a fresh encounter with the living God…The effectiveness of our ministry will flow out of who we are and who God has empowered us to be." (Wilson & Kronbach 2010, p.53)

When David, our Mission Pastor, asked me to lead and choose a team to care for our missionaries, my first thought was—choose the people carefully for this team. I'd seen our missionaries' sacrifices and challenges first hand and wanted a group who could really make a difference in their wellbeing. But who were these special volunteers? How was I to find them? Here is some criteria I used:

- Above all, what in their life already demonstrated a heart for missionaries? How had each one caught the desire to minister to our missionaries and where was that evidenced in their life?
- What qualities in their character were needed?
- What skills or experiences would be valuable to missionaries?

Following is our team at Trinity Church:

William caught the desire in graduate school as a student of psychology where he counseled with missionaries at a conference who were dealing with various issues. What? Missionaries have that kind of conflict which would interfere with their calling? He did his dissertation on what type of person would be more likely to succeed on the mission field (Britt 1980). William often gives up his vacation time to go halfway around the world to visit our missionaries and minister to them. He has a humility that shows. If you could put words to it, "Lord, my education, talents, time are yours; use them."

Paula's desire to care for missionaries came from her own personal experience as a medical missionary wife and mother, raising her kids in Trinidad. She has her master's degree in spiritual formation and has a vision to turn her home into a retreat for missionaries; a pretty clear indication of her heart for them. She lends the team the test of real life experiences, so she's good at seeing our ideas through "the field view." Would this really minister to families on the field or does it just look good to us as we sit here in church and talk about it?

Joan is a woman of prayer for our missionaries. Her concern for them is plainly evident when she shows up every Sunday to our missionary prayer group. She was there when our church sent out its very first missionary and acts to bring a long term historical perspective to our missionaries' lives and needs. As an added bonus she is a parent of one of our missionaries, so she knows firsthand the difficulty of leaving family behind.

Bill and Betty Jane were with Mission Aviation Fellowship (MAF) for years in Brazil. Bill was a pilot and safety officer, but often found himself talking with the missionaries he served about their struggles. He and his wife received a degree in counseling and spent the last ten years of their career developing the missionary care department at MAF. When talking to them about missionary needs, I often feel like they're shining a magnifying glass on things I cannot see as easily. Also, sometimes working with the mission agency can be delicate. Bill and Betty Jane helped us as we determined the different roles of agency and church, and to learn how to partner with the agency rather than work in isolation.

Sue is a retired missionary teacher, also with MAF, spending most of her adult life serving in challenging places such as Indonesia, Mexico,

Suriname and Haiti. Sue is one of the most giving and generous people I know to our missionaries. She and Betty Jane help them raise additional ministry support, an area that can be a real trial.

And me (**Linda**). Well, I caught the desire when I had an opportunity to minister as a family therapist at our denomination's missionary family camp in France. As I formed relationships with the single ladies who put themselves in dangerous immigrant neighborhoods to minister to women, I felt a strong desire to help those who made such sacrifices for Christ.

In summary, pray about and choose people who have a natural compassion for others and an ability to relate well with people. Do they already demonstrate a passion for missions and have either spiritual gifting, life experience or skills that would add valuable depth to the team? These may be competence, integrity, a vibrant prayer ministry, counseling, fundraising, short-term mission experience or a career in missions. Are they willing to invest the necessary time to connect with your missionaries, stay abreast of mission literature and/or attend an occasional missionary care conference, as well as some travel for field visits?

If your church is just starting out on the journey, it may be difficult to identify those who have a heart for missionaries. To get started, choose some who are spiritually mature and show compassion to others. Take them to a missionary care conference or better yet, go with them to visit one or two of your missionaries on the field to help them catch the vision.

Several years have passed since I had the privilege of watching God bring this team together. Speaking of the team to Trinity's missionaries, our Pastor once said "These people take very serious the business of caring for you." That means God is concerned about the wellbeing of His workers. He has already provided some in the body who have caught His desire to care for them. Ask God to direct you as you go and find them.

GET ON BOARD

1. Look around to see who in your church can relate well with others. Do their lives exhibit wise living and spiritual/emotional health?

2. From these, look for those who are already ministering to your missionaries through prayer, emailing, and networking their needs with others.

3. If they meet the first two criteria, choose those for your team who have training or experience in areas your missionaries need; counseling, support raising, business, missionary work. But beware of an elitist attitude where professionalism and training are your main criteria. As missionary caregivers point out, it is not only our competence but our character that is most essential in this work, and our dependence on God's direction.

Chapter 2

Philosophy Of Effective Ministry (POEM)

Linda Parker

Too much talky talky! When are we going to start caring for our missionaries? Joan saw our meeting get bogged down, again, in what she thought was a lot of unnecessary strategizing. I was helping the team to formulate our Philosophy of Effective Ministry (POEM), a written statement of what the Missionary Care Team of Trinity Church felt called by God to do. I had just come back from a team-building course at the Center for Intercultural Training (CIT) in North Carolina where I learned how instrumental the POEM can be to sharpen your focus as a team (see MindTheGaps.org for a current list of missionary training agencies). There are three components: 1) Our Purpose Statement is a one-sentence description of our mission. 2) Our Core Values serve as a guide to help us see that our actions and attitudes follow what we value most as we care for our missionaries. 3) Our goals and methods are specific ways we care for our missionaries that reveal our purpose and core values.

Joan wasn't the only one getting a little impatient. The three month process was remembered as long and tedious, but at times exciting as we sharpened our vision of what we were about. Not until later did we realize how helpful it would be.

We Don't Do That

David, our Mission Pastor had just created a missionary care team and he was excited about having a group of people involved with our missionaries to whom he could delegate a task. So, in one of our first meetings he waltzed in, handed us an evaluative tool and asked us to use it to help the church decide whether and how

> much to support a particular missionary. We all looked down at the evaluative tool and then handed it back to him. "That's not in our Philosophy of Ministry, Pastor David. We've decided in our core values to stay away from evaluative activities as much as possible. We want our missionaries to be free to discuss their needs with us without fear of how it will affect their support from the church. You'll have to find someone else to do this." Wow! We just told our Mission Pastor no and explained it in a way that he could accept.

Churches are busy places. There's much to do to further Christ's kingdom. But once word is out that there is a team of people to love and care for your missionaries, its only natural that many requests will come your way. The POEM is a Philosophy of *Effective* Ministry. You can do more effective ministry when you've thought through up front what God has called you to do, as well as what not to do!

So now, you're invited to board this train that will lead to your destination as a team — effective ministry to your missionaries. You need a trip plan (your POEM) to get you there, a guide that will keep you on track and ensures you'll make the important stops along the way.

DEVELOPING A PURPOSE STATEMENT

The first thing you need to do is decide where you're going and what you're trying to do. What do you hope to accomplish for your missionaries as you care for them? Your purpose statement will encapsulate in one or two sentences what you feel called to do.

Trinity Missionary Care Purpose Statement

> To promote the well-being, growth, effectiveness and sustainability of Trinity's career missionaries through facilitating the meeting of physical, spiritual and emotional needs.

We want our work to make a difference in their well-being, to see them and their families happy and fulfilled in what they are doing and growing closer to the Lord. It is important to see them grow spiritually, also to grow emotionally, able to handle stress and negative emotions in healthy ways. We also desire that they know their calling and be in a place that supports that calling. If they are effective at what God has called them to, they can withstand hardship; conversely, when they are not effective, even small challenges tend to become overwhelming. You may be reading this book because you feel the sadness of a missionary coming home prematurely. Ultimately our care must have the goal of sustainability. A way we best help our missionaries is to join with their agency to facilitate the meeting of physical, spiritual and emotional needs.

DETERMINING CORE VALUES

This brings us to our trip plan; our core values. When we're on a trip, it's not just getting where we're going that's important, but how we get there. What do you value the most as you travel down this track toward your destination? Are you interested in good, deep conversation or just a little peace and quiet to think? Do you like everything planned or would you rather just let things unfold spontaneously? Similarly, there are core values, non-negotiable principles that guide us in the way we care for our missionaries. They serve as a measuring stick so that what we are doing—our attitudes and actions—is in line with what we value the most. We narrowed down our core values to five:

Trinity Missionary Care Core Values

- Dependable care through grace-oriented relationships
- Fill gaps of needs not met by their mission agency
- Promote congregational awareness and involvement
- Encourage openness through assurance of secure communication
- Live congruently to build credibility

Establish Grace-oriented Relationships

A top priority for us is that everything we do has a positive effect on building grace-oriented relationships with our missionaries, the key to our ministry to them. These were not only relationships of the missionaries with us on the team, but with people in the church as well. We also wanted to emphasize a non-evaluative stance where our missionaries could open up to us without fear that it would affect their financial support.

Fill Gaps of Needs Not Met

More effective mission agencies have competent member care departments that do a good job taking care of their missionaries. Most churches, including ours, are not equipped to be the primary caretakers of their missionaries. However, our personal experience demonstrates that there are gaps of care. This can simply be because of the high ratio of missionaries to agency member care personnel. We think our missionaries deserve a second set of eyes to see their needs, more ears to listen, and extra hands to help.

> **Working Together**
> The care team received a "heads up" from the agency member care department of one of our missionaries. Our workers were in transition to another country and had a difficult time leaving. Would we be able to contact our missionaries and be a listening ear for them at this time? We were so grateful for an agency that valued the relationship we had with our missionaries so that we could give the extra support they needed for a good transition.

We envision church care teams communicating with agencies when they see needs that the agency should fill (i.e. more training in a certain area) and the agency contacting the church for needs that it is uniquely equipped to fill (i.e. practical needs while on home assignment, counseling needs if brought back from the field to work on major issues, or help with restoration after a moral failure). The effect of this type of collaboration between agency and church can yield huge dividends in the lives of our missionaries for His kingdom. See MindTheGaps.org to find a Restoration Care Plan Booklet which one mission agency uses when working with a church for restoration of its missionary.

Encourage Openness through Secure Communication

Missionaries are in the spotlight. They need some place they can be open when they're having trouble adjusting to another culture or have family issues without worrying about how that will affect their standing with the church. So we developed a policy of confidentiality.

But, confidentiality always has limits. Under what circumstances do we need to break confidentiality to get them or others the help they need? When do we notify the pastoral staff of something detrimental in their life and ministry? We knew we had to write a policy that was acceptable to the missionary, the mission agency and the pastoral staff, which was no small task. Chapter 3 shows our confidentiality policy and how we developed it.

Promote Congregational Awareness and Involvement

We wanted to use our team as a link between the missionary and people in the church. The flow of caring would be multiplied if it was not just from the few of us on the team, but also from many others in the church. One of our most successful endeavors to promote this core value was for each of our small groups to adopt a missionary family to keep in touch with, pray for and make them feel welcome when in town (see Chapter 8 for how this was developed). Again — more eyes to see, ears to listen and hands to help.

The Lone Ranger

I (Joan) was in charge of our "Birthday in a Box" project that enlists volunteers from the church to send a box full of gifts to each of our missionary kids. Since this was our first year, I was only able to sign up half of the needed volunteers to put together and send the boxes, so I decided to send the other half myself . . . until a team member reminded me of our core value of promoting congregational involvement. Then we brainstormed together ways we could recruit more volunteers from people in the church.

Live Congruently to Build Credibility

Credibility is so important when you say you care. Were we living out what we wanted to promote in our care for the missionaries? Were our relationships on the team growing in grace? Were we learning to be more effective as care providers? We adopted The Peacemaker Plan (Sande 2004 and PeaceMaker.net) as a method of conflict resolution for our team and became trained to use tools through Interpersonal Communication Programs that would find mutually satisfying solutions to issues that arose on the team (Miller, et.al, 2007 and CoupleCommunication.com). We also committed to sending two of our team members per year to a conference on missionary care to increase their effectiveness.

Take some time, ample time, to pray, discuss and write down your POEM. What has God called your team to do to care for its missionaries? After working on your trip plan, some on the team will probably say, like Joan, "Too much talky talky!" Don't worry. That's probably a sign that you're on the right track.

GET ON BOARD

You and your team have a unique set of gifts, experiences, talents and abilities that God has provided for you to care for your missionaries. Start with our POEM (see Trinity Church's Philosophy of Effective Ministry at the end of this chapter) and add, subtract or tweak it to fit your church.

1. At your next meeting, brainstorm about how to describe what you feel led by God to do to care for your missionaries in a one or two sentence purpose statement.

2. List your core values.

3. Taking into consideration the resources, abilities and experience of people on your team and in your church, list some goals, methods, and ways in which you will care for your workers. For example, maybe you have the same core value of promoting congregational involvement but your church doesn't have small groups to adopt each missionary. However, you do have someone who wants to use technology to connect people from the church with your missionaries. The goal for that core value might be to promote communication and understanding between missionary and congregation. That volunteer's use of technology is the method that gives footing to that goal.

See MindTheGaps.org for a collection of POEMS from other ministries.

PHILOSOPHY OF EFFECTIVE MINISTRY (POEM)

Trinity Missionary Care Team

PURPOSE STATEMENT

We exist for the glory of God to promote the well-being, growth, effectiveness and sustainability of Trinity Church's career missionaries through facilitating the meeting of physical, spiritual and emotional needs.

CORE VALUE 1 — Dependable care through grace-oriented relationships, with emphasis on a non-evaluative stance

Goal — Foster consistent, deep relationships between the care team and missionaries, so that they can be open about needs.

Methods

- Assign each missionary unit to a team member to build trusting relationships and keep in touch regularly and proactively learn about needs.
- Participate in short term mission trips to work with them in their ministries as well as to minister to them personally.
- Hold a retreat for missionaries who attend your annual mission conference to facilitate relationship building and ministry from the team and from each other.

CORE VALUE 2 — Fill gaps of needs not met by their mission agency

Goal — Develop a proactive care plan for them, taking into account needs not met by their mission agency.

Methods

- Contact member care personnel in their agency to ascertain gaps of care.

- Have a pre-field and post-field meal with missionaries to find out about home and field needs.
- Utilize the CSA (Cerny-Smith Adjustment Scale, CernySmith.com) to gain understanding of intercultural adjustment six months after they arrive on the field, when home on extended furlough, and before a field visit.

CORE VALUE 3 — Promote congregational awareness and involvement

Goal — Foster caring relationships between missionaries and small groups of people in the church

Methods

- Each family/individual will be adopted by a small group to keep in touch with them by email, phone or Skype at least once a month, pray for them and visit with them when home.
- When home at least two weeks or more, visit with the pastor and his wife.
- Develop a resource list of Trinity members who can meet professional or practical needs.

CORE VALUE 4 — Encourage openness through assurance of secure communication

Goal — Develop a policy of confidentiality that is acceptable to the missionary, agency and church staff.

Methods

- Review the confidentiality policy yearly or as needed to ensure it is followed.
- Gain regular feedback from missionaries regarding its effect on openness.

CORE VALUE 5 — Live congruently to build credibility

Goal — Nurture healthy Missionary Care Team relationships and equip the team for their task.

Methods

- Adopt the Peacemaker Plan as the care team's method of conflict resolution. Also train and use skills learned through Interpersonal Communication Programs.
- For teambuilding, utilize the DISC test (*InternalChange.com)* to understand how different team personalities work together effectively. Also have each team member "tell their story" to each other of God's work in their lives, including through pain. (For a description of these and other team building tools, see MindTheGaps.org.)
- Two team members a year will attend a conference on missionary care. Quarterly literature review at Team meetings.

Chapter 3

Confidentiality Policy

William Britt and Linda Parker

"It only takes one time where a missionary's confidentiality is violated for it to affect our reputation with the rest of our missionaries. They won't talk to us about their needs after that." This warning from one on our team echoed all of our thoughts as we reviewed how well our confidentiality policy had served our missionaries so far. We had established a policy early on as a result of our core value of secure communication, that is, a commitment to our missionaries not to share communication of a confidential nature with anyone outside the team. We realized then that we needed something written to hand to our missionaries, a policy and our pledge to follow it, that would give them the safety to open up to us (see Trinity Church's Missionary Care Team Confidentiality Policy at the end of this chapter).

We're inviting them into grace-oriented relationships with us. We want them not only to tell us about typical needs like needing a car to use on furlough, but also more vulnerable needs like team conflict, difficulties adjusting culturally, family issues, or questions of effectiveness in ministry. We want to be able to help before these difficulties (many of which are normal in mission life) rise to a level of affecting their wellbeing and work. Missionaries have fear that some in the church will misunderstand their struggles as an indication they are unable to do their work.

Much Ado About Something

I had severe anxiety over the health of a family member for a short period of time. We were in an isolated area with little accessible medical help. When I asked for prayer for this, it appeared to me that some in the church overreacted and lost confidence in my ability to do the work. It took some time to help people in the church see I could deal with the anxiety and move past it.

Having a care team of people who won't over interpret their struggles will increase a missionary's openness. But having a clear statement that those from the care team will keep things confidential will make it even more likely that this type of communication will take place.

LIMITS OF CONFIDENTIALITY

Realistically, there are limits to any confidentiality. Most states have laws for medical/mental health providers that if someone is harmful to themselves or others, information must be divulged in order to protect and arrange help for them. Though we as lay people on the care team are not often familiar with these laws of reporting, we decided to include these limits of confidentiality in our policy for ethical reasons. Most people can understand the need to break confidentiality for this reason. We recommend you check with local laws for mandated reporting in your state.

There was an additional consideration regarding limits unique to missionaries and their situation. Because our missionaries are sent out by our church, and work for an agency, we knew there might be other situations where our pastoral staff and/or the mission agency might need to be notified. We then consulted with our church pastors, our missionaries and their agencies to receive their input on these limits of confidentiality that were more unique to those in ministry. We saw a challenging task ahead to formulate a confidentiality policy that was acceptable to all three entities. Here are some issues we knew we had to deal with, as you may too.

The good, the bad and the ugly of the Church

- Because the church controls the missionary's support, he/she is less likely to open up to pastoral staff about problems.

- Some pastors are not good at keeping confidentiality.
- Pastors are pastoral. They want to be able to pray, protect, and utilize accountability to help their missionaries when major problems arise.
- Church staff are guardians of church resources and want to know if problems affect the missionary's ability to do the work they were sent out to do.
- Agencies have had bad experiences with some churches that have made them cautious about sharing information (i.e. churches that make unilateral decisions to bring a missionary home without contacting the agency).
- The trend is moving toward agencies partnering with churches to exchange information of a confidential nature. Agencies want to have a better relationship with the church so that they can communicate when major problems occur.
- A church care team must establish a high degree of trust with pastoral staff in order for them to trust the care team with information they don't have about the missionary.

Pastoral Staff Approval

When we met with our pastors, we wanted to know under what circumstances they wanted us to discuss confidential information with them regarding our missionaries. One hurdle we thought might come up was that the pastoral staff might want to know more than the missionary wanted them to know. On one hand, we knew how disconcerting it was for a pastor to suddenly hear that a missionary was coming home because of a problem that he knew nothing about. On the other hand, we knew how difficult it would be for the missionary if he thought that anything he talked with us about could be reported to his pastor. We had to resolve the tension between these two valid concerns of the missionary and our pastors. Similarly, how comfortable were the pastors with the care team knowing more about their missionaries than they? We were pleased to find out that our pastors heartily supported confidentiality between the care team and the church's missionaries. They merely wanted to be notified by the Mission Pastor if there was a problem severe enough to affect their personal or family life or their ability to do their work.

When we communicated this back to our missionaries, they felt this was a reasonable limit to their confidentiality with us. We were pleased that it was easy to find agreement and attribute our success here to the wisdom and godly maturity of our pastors and missionaries, but also, the ability of our care team to establish trust with the pastoral staff. The high standards we used to select our care team went a long way to help pastors relinquish control of information.

Input from Mission Agencies

We emailed all of our missionaries' agencies, letting them know we wanted to work with them on the care of our missionaries, and that we were formulating a policy of confidentiality. We felt it was important for the mission agency, ourselves and the missionary to know under what conditions we should divulge information of a confidential nature from our missionaries, as well as receive it from the agency. That way, if a crisis came up, those procedures would be in place and could be acted upon easily with no one being offended. It would also make it more likely that agency and church would not be duplicating efforts.

We found that rather than send emails or letters to overwhelmed agencies it was better to contact them by phone or talk with them at conferences. As we developed relationships with our missionaries' agencies they became more responsive to our working together on confidentiality.

Missionary Endorsements

We received input from our missionaries throughout this process, since they were the people for whom the policy was developed. There are two limits of confidentiality which are not professional, but ethical:

- When a missionary or his family was a danger to himself or others and needed help or protection (i.e. child or spousal abuse or suicidal/homicidal threat), we would request that the missionary contact the appropriate authorities that could help, in our presence. This might be the agency, mission pastor, and local emergency services. We immediately make sure the missionary receives help.

- If there was incapacitation in functioning or family life such that they couldn't do their work (moral failure, marital crisis, addiction or depression), we asked that they contact their mission agency and our Mission Pastor regarding the problem for the purpose of getting help and accountability, and we would notify both their agency and our Mission Pastor that they would be calling. We believe it is healthier to give the missionaries the opportunity to face the issue by making the call themselves.

After formulating the first draft we showed it to some of our missionaries and asked them if the policy helped them feel free to open up to us. Also, we asked if the situations where we felt it was necessary to break confidentiality seemed reasonable to them. The answer to both questions was a resounding yes. They felt more freedom to share things with us, and they wanted their pastors and mission agencies to know about extreme situations where they needed help, protection or accountability.

Some have advised that we have the missionary sign the policy. We do not do that in our current practice, but you may want to if your church sees the need for that.

Delicate Situations

Still, even with a policy in place, the nature of ministry in the church is such that your care team will feel the pull to compromise your commitment to confidentiality. For example, people who know that you have just visited a missionary on the field may want to know how they are doing. Maybe they want to pray more specifically for them, or maybe their motives are not so pure. If you sense they're genuine in their concern, how do you answer them to honor that concern as well as the missionary's right to privacy, especially if one of your core values is to increase congregational involvement? We find it is immensely helpful to ask the missionaries themselves when they are giving us information of a confidential nature what they would like us to communicate to those who ask about them from the church, and especially, what they would like us not to say.

Another situation which may derail the train of secure communication is when you travel with your pastor on a short term trip. Some of your experiences may be with pastors who would be offended to be excluded from certain conversations with the missionary. This is where you can see how important it is to have a policy agreed upon up front by everyone.

> **Meet Without Me**
> David, our Mission Pastor said, "The Care Team is welcome to let me know when I don't need to be part of a conversation. I'm not offended because I know how important confidentiality is to the team's ability to learn of our missionaries' needs so that they can minister to them. I will have my own special time of ministry with them."

Freedom to be Broken

As a team, we take our missionaries away for a day or two, as a gift for coming to our annual mission's conference. This gives them a chance to focus on their relationship with the Lord without any obligations, and to be encouraged by us as a team and by each other. It's a special time where we get to know each other and pray for one another on a deeper level. After one particularly open sharing time, one of them said, "This is the first time since becoming a missionary that I've felt free, in a church context, to share this." This was probably not reflective of our peoples' lack of approachability since our church is blessed with a particularly grace-oriented congregation and pastoral staff. It's probably more a function of the larger Christian culture that still sees brokenness and weakness as an aberration rather than the normal experience of most of us through which God shows His power and glory. And yes, in a perfect Christian world there probably would be no need for confidentiality since we would all accept each other in our brokenness. You may say yes and amen! It is true that you as a care team can gain your missionaries' trust and openness by being people who are approachable and understand the normalcy of brokenness, even in your own lives. But as we live within the realities of a world that may not be as understanding, an assurance of secure communication is essential.

We like to review the policy once a year, or as needed (for example, after visiting missionaries on the field). How well are we following the policy? Are our missionaries remaining open with us about their more vulnerable needs? Were there any activities where the lines of confidentiality were crossed? The scrutiny is well worth the effort because, after all, it only takes one time where a missionary's confidentiality is violated to tarnish our reputation. Let's keep that place of cherished trust real so ministry can take place.

GET ON BOARD

1. Have someone on your care team meet with the key players in your church that should be consulted regarding a policy of confidentiality. If a professional counselor is not already on your care team, ask someone from the church that understands confidentiality to attend the meeting as an advisor. You can start with our confidentiality policy and tweak it to fit your church's situation.

2. Show the first draft to some of your missionaries and ask them whether this policy would make them feel safe to open up to the care team regarding their needs and whether they felt the pastors' request to divulge certain information was reasonable.

3. If there is disagreement, then possibly ask a representative from both entities (the missionaries and the pastoral staff) to meet, discuss their differences and come up with the appropriate wording.

4. Regarding agencies, contact the ones with whom you have a particularly close relationship. Find the name(s) of the key person(s)

involved in missionary care in that agency and call them personally. Tell them of your desire to have a confidentiality policy in place that is mutually satisfying to all three entities: missionary, agency and church. Then ask for the agency's confidentiality policy. If the differences are minimal, ask if both your church and the agency can follow your church's policy, and write a follow-up email regarding the agreement. Give the final policy to all pastoral staff.

5. Finally, the next time you meet with each of your missionaries, hand them the written Confidentiality Policy for their review. Ask them to read it and tell you their feelings about it. Hopefully, you will have a positive response. If not, go back to the drawing board.

CONFIDENTIALITY POLICY

MISSIONARY CARE TEAM, TRINITY CHURCH

The following confidentiality agreement will be in effect for all interaction between Trinity Church's missionaries and the members of the Missionary Care Team.

• • • •

All communication of a confidential nature with the members of the Missionary Care Team is confidential. We want you to be able to talk with us openly about your needs so that we may be of help. The only times we will break this agreement of confidentiality are as follows:

- When a dangerous situation arises (examples: child, spouse, elder abuse, suicidal/homicidal threat, gravely disabled), we will ask you to report this to the appropriate sources of help, your agency and the Mission Pastor immediately, when possible in our presence. If upon immediate follow-up we find you are unable or unwilling to report it, we will do so ourselves.
- When we see that personal struggles significantly interfere with one's work role and/or ability to function (possible examples could be major depression, marital crisis, addiction behaviors or moral failure), we will encourage you to inform a trusted person in your agency leadership and the Mission Pastor for the purposes of gaining support and accountability. We will also let your agency leadership and the Mission Pastor know you will be calling.

When we feel the need to consult with others about your situation, we will ask your permission.

PART TWO

Passenger List

Choosing Who You Send

Introduction

David Wilson

In his book *Leading from the Sandbox,* Tim Addington identifies *ambiguity* as a major dysfunction of any organization. He says, "Most ministries have never identified the central ministry focus they must concentrate on day in and day out...Ambiguity about these core issues makes it very difficult to achieve any kind of organizational alignment... And team members find it difficult to know how to make good decisions or focus efforts." (Addington 2010, 56)

For the missionaries on your care list, this means that they need to fit somehow into the larger strategic focus of the church. If they do not fit, they will likely become high maintenance and cause extra work for your team. Many times a friend or relative of a church member comes into the church and presents a mission proposal, and because of the relationship, he/she is added to the missionary support list. Over time, the missionary role is filled with these types of additions and it bears no resemblance to the unified vision of the church. The person who introduced the missionary to the church at the beginning may move away over time and then church leadership begins to evaluate the budget. Those who are unknown to the larger body are the first to be cut. This is a harsh reality and it is very unfair for the missionary on the field who is still serving the Lord, but must now look for support again.

To illustrate this point, if a church has a very strong church planting/evangelistic focus, but the missionary is engaged in the work of social justice/poverty alleviation, then conflicts will be inherent in the relationship. The church will frequently ask, "What are you doing to share the gospel and start churches?" On the other hand, the missionary will often be disappointed when he/she asks for special funds for a project and is turned down since it does not fit the evangelistic goals of the church.

There are many books available which can help your church and/or mission team discover its unique calling. Addington's book *Leading from the Sandbox* is a great start. However, for the purposes of church based missionary care teams, use the four C's when considering missionary candidates to ensure that the whole church will be fully engaged in caring from the very beginning:

> **Competence** — Beware of the words "I'm not good at anything else, so I think God is calling me to be a missionary." The last thing the kingdom of God needs is people sent out from churches to be missionaries out of pity.
>
> **Character** — This is the toughest to discern with just an interview meeting. William Britt's chapter on predicting missionary success will help your team with due diligence through references and a variety of testing.
>
> **Culture** — The missionary must fit the sending church's strategic focus or else they will not be able to relate to the church's mission strategy. Chapter five will walk you through several "what if" scenarios to help stimulate your thinking on this.
>
> **Calling** — Be alert for a strong calling because when things start going wrong, the Lord's call on their life will be what keeps them on the field (Hay 2007, 110).

Chapter four will address Competence and Character, and chapter five will address Culture and Calling. At first glance, these may not seem like applicable topics to include in a book about missionary care, but without clear alignment between a church and its missionaries, there will be frustrations, hurt feelings and undue strain for your care team. Hopefully, these two chapters will give your team perspective as you seek to care for your global workers.

Chapter 4

Predictors of Missionary Success

William Britt

Competence and character are difficult to assess for any sending church. The first issue is choosing what competencies and character traits are needed in an overseas setting, which is much different than choosing a missionary for your own sending church culture. The second issue is whether the missionary care team should even be involved in the selection process, given that choosing missionaries is an evaluative process that may make it difficult later for the care team to take on the role of caring for those who were asked to wait, or to make changes in their lives before being sent overseas.

We have resolved the second issue by having a Missions Committee that does evaluation, freeing the care team to focus on care. The Missions Committee in our church, designated by the Elder Board, makes policy decisions, selects missionary candidates for approval, and determines the funding they will receive. The Missionary Care Team is a subsidiary of the Missions Committee. In your church, the Pastor, the Mission Pastor or the church board might be the ones who select missionary candidates.

Many agencies are very good in performing evaluations, but others have varying degrees of ability to select, while "pass through" agencies leave it up to the church to choose the missionary, and they just handle administration. If an agency is going to do the selection, how does the church know whether their candidate will qualify? It could be very disheartening to the candidate and the church to have this person rejected by an agency.

We believe "due diligence" must be done by both the church and the mission agency in making sure the candidate has the best chance to succeed, and the church must bear a greater responsibility if the mission agency has a weak selection process. Therefore, the church must have a key role in vetting the missionary candidates being sent overseas. In this chapter, we will explain our process and show how we carry out this important function at Trinity Church. Then, whoever takes on this evaluative role in your church will have some "tracks to run on" as we mind the gaps together.

MISSIONARY CANDIDATE EVALUATION PROCESS

The first step for someone in our church to start the process of becoming a missionary is to have an interview with the Mission Pastor. He evaluates the call of the applicant, if the person has an idea of agency and location to serve, if the call fits with the strategic focus of our church, and if the applicant asks that our church be his sending church.

If the applicant passes this first step of the process, we ask him to complete an application, which includes references. When received, he is interviewed by the Missions Committee to determine if they could support him based upon call, vision and type of service. If the committee believes he is a viable candidate, then a subgroup of the committee vets the agency he has selected, and refers him to a psychologist for further evaluation.

The psychologist is given a copy of the references, does an interview with the applicant, and administers psychological testing. Elements from the interview, references, and psychological tests known from research (Britt, 1980) to predict missionary success overseas are evaluated using a multiple regression formula. The psychological report combining all the above data is sent to the subgroup indicating recommendations, including whether the applicant is likely to rank as Most Successful, More Successful, Less Successful, or Least Successful (these four levels will be explained later in this chapter). It is important to note that the prediction formula is only one part of the total psychological assessment used to produce the psychological report. The psychologist relies on clinical judgment, candidate history, interpretation of psychological tests, and interview data to produce that final report.

If the subgroup agrees that the mission agencies' goals fit with the strategic focus of the church mission plan, is doctrinally sound, provides human resource personnel to care for the missionary, and has sound fundraising and retirement policies, then the agency can be approved. The subcommittee makes a recommendation to the full Missions Committee, taking into account the mission agency selected and the Psychological Report. They also make a recommendation regarding the amount of support the applicant will be given based on previously established Missions Committee criteria (see MindTheGaps.org for a Matrix that is used for selection).

The Committee votes to either support the missionary for the amount recommended as a sending church, or advise further training, and character development. If support is chosen, the applicant is sent to the Elder Board with a packet explaining the Committee's decision and requesting an interview and final decision.

Is it possible to predict who might be more or less successful in cross-cultural service? Based upon a composite drawn from research (Britt, 1980) on successful and unsuccessful cross-cultural workers, a fascinating picture can be drawn, although it won't fit everyone exactly. The study used 111 participants, the entire population of the Agape Movement of Campus Crusade for Christ. Success was measured using a Success Inventory developed by the leadership of the Agape Movement and used for evaluation of each cross-cultural worker by the continental director and other leadership. Seventy-six variables from the application, references, field interview and psychological test assessment were entered into a multiple regression statistical analysis which yielded twelve (12) predictor variables, which are available in a prediction equation to help with candidate selection.

First, a legitimate question must be answered. How can you use research done in the late 1970's to predict success when our culture and the candidates produced by it have changed so drastically? A recent research article addressed this issue by asking if it is legitimate to throw out all past research and just use research of the past few years, as if somehow peoples' personality traits and human nature completely change every few years. It has taken decades of cross-cultural research to determine the five personality factors that each human shares regardless of culture: Openness, conscientiousness, extraversion, agreeableness, and neuroticism. Current research always builds on past research, and although new factors are discovered, they rarely invalidate what was discovered years before, especially in the field of human personality.

If this argument were true that past discoveries of human personality become invalid every few decades, then we would have to measure what the Bible says about our human character by the same standard, and would need new revelation every few decades to keep up with our changing human nature. What was true of people successfully or unsuccessfully navigating a cross-cultural experience in decades past is highly likely to still be true, although new studies utilizing current missionaries in the changing receptor world need to be done. Until then, in the absence of more current research, the findings should be used only as one part of the entire evaluation process, taking into account the sending/receiving world changes. A least/less successful predicted outcome should serve as an impetus for more in depth evaluation of the candidate.

Portrait of the Most Successful Missionary

The most successful missionary would possess good work habits and have an ability to control anxiety in an appropriate way. People depend on this individual to organize things and get the job done, and are seldom disappointed. The missionary is very adaptable to new situations, no matter how ambiguous they might seem. The ability to cope with ambiguity is an essential missionary trait.

Persons observing this missionary rarely see her exhibiting moodiness or severe depression, but report that she tends to be steady emotionally. She comes across as somewhat polished and socially aware, with good insight into herself and others. She tends to be more interested in keeping a group of people unified and working together than in getting her opinion across on every subject. Feeling at ease with others and relating well to them, she has an ability to read the subtle cultural cues and adapt herself to them, not feeling a need to pronounce this custom right or that one wrong. She is not so locked into her American culture that she cannot adapt to the new one.

When her supervisor asks her to do a task, she will pause to consider the request and give some input to the supervisor if she feels it is either unnecessary or if she senses conflict or would be overworked. When things do not go as planned, she may feel upset, but generally prays about it and perseveres.

This missionary is more likely to be firstborn, under 31, male or female, single or married, without children or with a small family. The father would have been in the home most of the time prior to the candidate's 15th birthday.

Portrait of the Least Successful Missionary

In contrast, the least successful missionary tends to be very controlled, socially precise, and compulsive about doing things. Others observe him to be very rigid, and sense a lack of creativity and flexibility.

He has a difficult time with the ambiguities of the new culture, and people hear him complain of being depressed or "down" frequently. He seems unable to control his anxious feelings, and becomes upset at customs in this new culture that are different from the way "things should be done."

He tells people he is more of a loner, and has difficulty getting to know new people. However, people tend to like him because he seems so humble and accommodating. He will do almost anything asked of him; the first to admit difficulty saying "no." When things don't go as planned, he doesn't seem to become outwardly upset, just shrugs and says he will "trust God." Yet his mood seems to change and he tends to feel depressed. After awhile he might get disproportionately angry over a small matter and feel confused as to why he acted this way.

In groups, he has a difficult time because he has to let everyone know his opinion about each issue. Sometimes he becomes so emotionally involved in an issue that to disagree with him is perceived as a personal attack. At times, the nationals have been very offended by some of his blunt remarks.

Demographically, he is probably a last born, mid 30's male or female with several children. There is a good possibility he lost his father prior to his 15th birthday, either through death or divorce.

It should be stressed that these two vignettes are hypothetical, no one person completely fitting either.

Explanation of the Predictors

These composites are based on predictors of success drawn from the 16 PF (a psychological test), the psychological interview, and items that have been incorporated into the references. Mission agencies differ in their ability to provide good evaluations, and we "mind the gaps" by making sure our candidates are likely to be 'more' or 'most' successful rather than "least" successful.

Underlying the predictors in these composites are years of research on cross-cultural workers in missions, the Peace Corps, military, etc. which were further validated on missionaries in this research study mentioned earlier. Using them will render objectivity to selection of candidates rather than just guessing at what might be helpful. It also might prevent some tragic, painful, and premature returns from the field, as well as cost to the mission agency and church.

All twelve predictors accounted for 56% percent of the variation in success. This means that if 100 things accounted for all the success of a missionary, these predictors account for 56 of them, the other 44 being unknown. According to one study, accounting for one third to one half of the variation in success internationally would be an achievement. Thus, all twelve must be used to maximize predictive power. The predictor equation is presented on MindTheGaps.org for use by the person who has access to the needed data.

PREDICTORS IN RANK ORDER FOR PREDICTION EQUATION

Predictor 1: Undisciplined vs. Controlled

Variance: 9%

Source: Factor Q3, 16PF

Definition: The ability to control anxiety

Ratings of Response		Less/least	More/most successful
1-Low:	lacks control	9-High-controlled end	6-7 -Just above average
10-High:	controlled socially precise compulsive		

More/most successful — A missionary who is rated as being moderately high tends to possess good work habits and keeps his emotions somewhat controlled. He can be depended on to organize things and get the job done. It is likely that the need for this type of person on the mission field has not changed over the decades.

Less/least successful — One who is extremely high on this predictor tightly controls anxiety, with too much obsessiveness and rigidity. Creativity and flexibility are diminished, and she becomes intolerant of ambiguity and disorder in her life. It is easy to see what a difficult time she would have in the ambiguous environment of another culture.

Predictor 2: Moodiness

Variance: 7%

Source: Reference Trait

Ratings of Response	Less/least	More/most successful
1-Never or rarely apparent	closer to often apparent	closer to never
2-Sometimes apparent		
3-Often apparent		

In order for this trait to be observed by people who know him well, he would have to exhibit overt changes in mood over a period of time.

Predictor 3: Birth Order

Variance: 5%

Source: Application Biographic Data

Ratings of Response	Less/least	More/most successful
1-Firstborns	Least: Lastborns	More: Middle children
2-Middle children	Less: Firstborns	Most: Firstborns
3-Lastborns		

Caution should be used in isolating this factor from the twelve, but other research has shown this to be a robust finding.

Predictor 4: Forthright vs. Astute

Variance: 5%

Source: Factor N, 16PF

Ratings of Response	Less/least	More/most successful
1-Low: Forthright	3-4: closer to Forthright	5-6: closer to Astute
10-High: Astute		

More successful — Someone who is slightly more polished and socially aware, a bit more insightful regarding themselves and others. She is somewhat more interested in promoting calm in a group than getting her opinions across, and is likely to be more attuned to subtle cultural cues.

Less successful — Someone who is genuine, but may come across more bluntly in another culture and have less self-insight, which may mean less sensitivity to cultural mores and less ability to perceive how he is coming across, offending nationals by his more critical and assertive attitude.

Predictors 5 & 6: Age & Family Size

Variance: 5% & 7%

Source: Application Biographic Data

Ratings of Response	Less/least	More/most successful
Age & Family Size	Less: Age <41; Least: Age <51 [mean age at entry with large family]	More: Age <36; Most: Age< 31 [mean age at entry with small family]

Age is highly correlated with family size. Both corroborate the finding by Williams (1973) study of Wycliffe staff that younger married missionaries who tend to have no or smaller families at the entry level were more successful than older ones with larger families at entry. These predictors are likely sensitive to the fact that those younger entry-level missionaries are generally more flexible and adaptable, not having families to concern them. Change is more disruptive for those who are older with families going overseas for the first time who have developed a settled lifestyle.

Predictor 7: Relates to Others

Variance: 4%

Source: Interview Question: "How do you feel you relate to others?"

Ratings of Response	Less/least	More/most successful
1-Enjoys being with others 2-(a less enthusiastic response) 3-Takes a while to get to know me or I tend to be a loner	3-Tends to be a loner	1-Enjoys being with others

It is fairly obvious that a missionary who does not relate well to others is going to have a difficult time in ministry and with her team.

Predictor 8: Response to Authority

Variance: 4%

Source: Reference Question: "How does he/she respond to authority?"

Ratings of Response	Less/least	More/most successful
1-Outstanding, servant's heart	1-Outstanding, servant's heart	More: 2-Good, fine
2-Good, fine		
3-Difficulty working with at times (has questioned authority, has questioned directions, but goes ahead)		

This finding is rather surprising, because those applicants whose referents respond "outstanding, with a servant's heart" tend to be less successful than those whose referents respond "good, fine." Evidently, more successful missionaries tend to respond to authority a little less enthusiastically. Although difficult to untangle, perhaps those who make an impression on a referent with how "servant-like" they are, do not have the leadership and assertive qualities needed in international service. They may be a bit too accommodating, passive and dependent. Maybe this predictor is sorting out leaders from followers.

Predictor 9: Social Poise

Variance: 3%

Source: Reference Trait

Ratings of Response	Less/least	More/most successful
1-Excellent, above average	1-Excellent	2-Average
2-Average		
3-Below Average		

This is another surprising finding that those rated excellent tend to be less successful than those who are average. Because this measure is not defined in the Reference Questionnaire, it is difficult to know exactly what this finding means. Perhaps applicants who impressed referents enough to be marked high on social poise were a bit too fastidious for a different culture where American cultural norms and expectations were not observed, and the missionaries became upset at the failure of nationals to "do it the right way."

Predictor 10: Perseverance/Self-Discipline

Variance: 3%

Source: Reference Trait

Ratings of Response	Less/least	More/most successful
1-Excellent, above average	4-Below average	1-Excellent, above average
2-Average		
3-Below average		

This has been noted in other studies as a strong predictor of success versus early termination. This variable best discriminated the most successful from all the others, with referents rating them Excellent more often. Although a weaker predictor in this study, it separates those who have the discipline to be strong in persevering through the difficulties encountered overseas.

Predictor 11: Flexibility vs. Rigidity

Variance: 3%

Source: Interview Question: "How do you react when things do not go as planned?"

Ratings of Response	Less/least	More/most successful
1-Trust God	1-Trust God	2-Pray about it, or
2-Pray about it	(rated above average)	3-May upset me at first
3-May upset me at first		

Less successful: This predictor may be uncovering a tendency to deny hurt or anger when things do not go as planned, responding with the more conventional answer "trust God."

More successful: In contrast, those who are able to recognize their disappointment enough to pray about it or feel upset adjust better than those who do not admit frustration. They may appear more flexible, but are actually defensive or hide their true response. The implication is there may be a process involved in being flexible, and if a person must deny disappointment or the need to pray, they tend to be less successful.

Predictor 12: Father Absence

Variance: 2%

Source: Application Biographic Data

Definition: Any 5-year period of father absence from the home before 15th birthday

Ratings of Response	Less/least	More/most successful
1- 10 to 15 yrs	Father absence	No father absence
2- 6 to 10 yrs	as defined	as defined
3- 0 to 5 yrs		

This was included in this study because Peace Corps research in the 1960's found it to be a strong predictor of those Peace Corp volunteers who were most successful versus those who had to return home due to emotional problems. Even though it accounts for only 2% of the variance, it was present for all of those in the Least Successful group.

This predictor may be more important now than when this study was done, because father absence is more prevalent in our culture. If the study were replicated, there may be a much higher incidence of father absence in the sample studied. Fathers typically model more instrumental behavior, inviting children to join them in the world, making it seem a safe place to experience. The absence of this role model may make it more difficult for missionaries to adjust to the demands and overcome the fears of a new culture.

HOW TO USE THE PREDICTORS

The first step is to make sure all 12 predictors are available for use from their appropriate instrument. The demographic predictors, birth order, age, family size, and father absence can be determined from the application or can be asked in the Psychological Interview.

The interview predictors should be included on the interview form that either the psychologist uses in the Psychological Interview or someone from the church selection team uses in evaluating the applicant. These ratings are subjective, with typical responses provided as guides from the Field Interviews actually used by Campus Crusade for Christ (now Cru) Agape Staff to interview their candidates. We have taken these key questions identified by this study and included them in our Psychological Interview administered by the psychologist (see MindTheGaps.org for a copy of our psychological interview).

The 16PF would need to be administered by a psychologist and the scale scores provided to whoever is going to use the prediction formula.

The reference questionnaires that are sent out to referents for the applicant should contain the questions and trait rating scale noted in the table above. Then the ratings for each predictor from the reference questionnaires would need to be averaged in order to come up with the number for that predictor that is to be entered in the Predictor Equation.

The numbers from all 12 are entered into the Predictor Equation, which yields a number close to 1, 2, 3 or 4: 1-Least Successful; 2-Less Successful; 3-More Successful; 4-Most Successful. The most powerful prediction is to then categorize the applicant as either Less Successful=1-2 and Most Successful=3-4. (see MindTheGaps.org for the prediction equation)

The most important issue is that to account for 56% of the variance, all twelve must be used, with none used in isolation. The most important predictors are listed first in descending order in the equation.

These predictors, which are part of the Psychological Assessment report from the psychologist, which also includes the Psychological

Interview and interpretation of test results, when combined with our assessment of call and evaluation of the application and references, has sometimes resulted in our saying "no" or "wait" to a candidate when the agency has said "yes." Although this may seem cold and heartless, we had rather say "wait" until issues have been worked out than see our people go into international service only to return crushed and embarrassed that they "failed" in their mission service. This attitude is born of these failure experiences that occurred before we began this more rigorous assessment.

FOR FURTHER CONSIDERATION

In context of these predictors of success, there are a few caveats which we would like to mention. First is determining a definition for success. Churches and agencies alike have struggled with this concept for many years. Some may gauge success by the numbers: churches being planted, tracts being distributed, baptisms of converts, etc. Others may use a more subjective method by seeking feedback from field leaders to determine the faithfulness of the work and the accomplishments of tasks (useful for pilots, translators, administrative roles, etc). For the purposes of this chapter, success is determined by having a thriving ministry, regardless of the goals of that ministry.

Second, we realize that Father Absence is a difficult topic and that each year this becomes a larger and more pervasive condition in our western culture. As a result, the percentage of missionary applicants with a father absence continually increases year after year. The data clearly demonstrates a correlation, but there are additional factors that should be considered. Perhaps some follow-up questions can be asked of candidates, such as: "Who filled the role of a father figure in your life?" "Who taught you what it was like to be a man?" Or for a woman, "How did you learn to relate in healthy ways to men?" "Who is a model for a healthy marriage?" Even though father absence continues to increase, human beings are resilient and often find coping mechanisms and alternate strategies to overcome family system dysfunctions. You should never rule someone out based on this predictor, or any other predictor, in isolation. They must be used in concert for best results.

Third, there are a variety of roles in the modern missionary movement where some traits are more desired in the candidate. For aviation pilots, translators and accountants, the qualified candidate needs to be more on the control side without a high tolerance for differences. Always be prepared to consider the job qualifications for the person and not just rely exclusively on the scores and results of the test instrument.

Fourth, the predictors of success is an instrument that is used to provide a point in time prediction of how this individual will fare internationally if nothing changes. God's people have always been able to adapt, change and overcome every obstacle placed before them. Consider Moses and his calling to lead God's people out of Egypt. It took forty years in the desert, but God used that time to shape him into a useful shepherd of His people. Likewise, Paul was in training for nearly 17 years before he was able to realize his ministry and calling. More than anything, this instrument should not be used as a qualifying/disqualifying tool, but more of an assessment device that will help to highlight areas that need attention.

CONCLUSION

Estimates suggest millions of dollars are spent each year on inferior work and premature return of missionaries, money which could be better used to further the kingdom. The lesson learned for our team has been a little preventive work up front is far less costly emotionally and financially than failure later due to fear of offending our candidates or mission agencies. Of the four C's (Competence, Character, Calling and Culture), competence and character are the most difficult to assess and discern. We have chosen "Predictors of Missionary Success" as our guide through this difficult process. This requires someone who is willing to put in the time, energy and effort as well as the expertise for proper evaluation. In your church, you may have another tool at your disposal, but you must not neglect thoughtful evaluation of a candidate's competence and character. When considering missionary candidates, ensure that the missionary care team is fully engaged in caring from the very beginning, and provide due diligence through references and testing for the sake of the kingdom.

GET ON BOARD

1. Is there a trained and skilled psychologist in your church whom you can engage to evaluate missionary candidates? Is there someone in your community who can serve in this capacity? Is there a school of Christian psychology near you which could help?

2. Do you know of another tool for evaluating character and competence that you could employ?

3. As you learn about the "Predictors," do you see patterns which have emerged in your current missionary family which are explained by this assessment tool?

Chapter 5

Strategic Focus of the Church

Bill & Betty Jane Born and David Wilson

The last words of Jesus, as he was ascending to heaven in Acts 1:8 provide a clear vision for being strategic in everything we do as a church. He said, "…you will be my witnesses in Jerusalem, and in all Judea and Samaria, and to the ends of the earth." Clearly, our task is to share the good news of the gospel both locally and globally. The specifics of the local and global strategy for each church are unique. This strategy is principally developed from historical and current endeavors in which the congregation has been involved, reflecting the missionaries and agencies which are supported by the congregation. Naturally, it need not be limited, as your vision expands, and may include other ministries, countries or missionaries as long as it fits within your church's own unique strategic focus.

Even if the term is not used, many churches have a "strategy"; a calling and a culture or style of ministry. The strategy may be eclectic if it has freely developed, unguided over the years. The focus will look different in each church. For example, targeting unreached people groups has been a popular method of engaging the whole church in a mission endeavor and is a good way to get started. The U.S. Center for World Missions in Pasadena, California, defines the unreached as *"a people group among which there is no indigenous community of believing Christians with adequate numbers and resources to evangelize their people without outside / cross-cultural assistance"* (USCWM.org). If you are passionate for this area of ministry, you may likely find others in the congregation who are equally concerned for the unreached as well, maybe even someone who is called to go. The Spirit often works that way.

Churches have a variety of strengths given by the Spirit to minister. If your church is "doing" mission without a carefully planned strategy, first identify the strengths of your missionaries and congregation and start there. Should you wish to broaden the impact of your current strategy, prayerfully consider how to introduce and develop a new area of impact. There is no hurry to change your strategy quickly since churches are much more reticent to changes than individuals. Predetermining a slow but consistent pace toward change will yield the best results. A hurried approach may undo your chances of success. Consider identifying candidates with a passion for both local and global mission from within your own church. If you find no ready interest, consider partnering with missionaries from your denomination or ask local pastors regarding missionaries they have sent and join them in their endeavor. Request a representative from a sending agency with that mission thrust to come to your church for a dialogue with your leaders. The agency may know of someone nearby for you to support. The rationale for choosing someone locally is the advantage of more opportunity to visit with your missionary during a furlough. You are also better able to care for them without the constraints of a short visit as they pass through.

We are seeking to set up an ideal relationship between our church, a mission agency and a missionary family. As we study the relationship between our return on investment (ROI) and our church's strategic focus we want to maximize the effectiveness of our missionaries. One of the ways effectiveness can be undercut is when they are not aligned with the mission of the sending church.

Our church took several years to introduce a new ministry to a specific country in a region of interest. First, our mission leadership team prayed for vision and direction. We informed the denomination of the new vision God had put on our heart. The following year we invited a national pastor from that region, who was well known to our denominational leadership, as the keynote speaker of our mission conference. Following the conference, we formed cross-generational short-term mission teams from the congregation and sent two teams a year to minister there during the next few years. Deep relationships were made with believers in the region and momentum built gradually for the new project. We commissioned each team in the Sunday morning worship service before they departed. A daily blog of team activity was posted on the church's website. Shortly after their return, each team gave a report to the congregation while the excitement, testimonies and photos were still current.

Not only were our short-term team members energized, the passion also spread to those who financially and prayerfully supported their efforts. In His providence, God provided us with a believer from that country studying in a local university to befriend our mission team and church family, even to accompany several of the short-term teams. This was a definite indication of His pleasure and encouragement in the new direction which we added to our mission outreach.

With a mission strategy in place, the church stands ready to prayerfully choose missionary candidates. There are young people in the high school or college ministries interested in becoming a missionary, so we interview them as early as possible to hear their hearts, pray for them, encourage them, guide their training, and assist them to go to mission conferences like Urbana conference. Greg Carter has developed curriculum for churches to use to develop the skills, knowledge and character for missionary candidates in a church environment (Carter 2010).

Our church attempts to send many of our interested college students to Urbana, the Intervarsity Christian Fellowship student mission conference, which is held every three years between Christmas and New Years. Today's students still seek careers that will make a difference in the world. Many careers of kingdom impact are solidified at Urbana by students. Whether or not college students choose a mission career, they return with an expanded global perspective and new interest in praying for and supporting mission endeavors of the church.

Pastors receive more requests for missionary support than any church could possibly fund. The beauty of a mission strategy is that it provides discernment as you choose which requests to seriously consider. Prayerfully pursue a relationship with those whose ministry already matches your mission thrust. Members of your congregation will also introduce you to missionaries they know, providing personal insight into someone you may consider because of their personal connection.

As former missionaries, we are passionate about a church seriously considering their own members who present themselves for mission service. Often they have been nurtured by the church since the cradle and made many of their significant spiritual decisions within the context of the local church's ministry. Some have met the Lord as adults and have been discipled by friends and neighbors who are members in the local church. Their best contacts for prayer and financial support are peers, Sunday school teachers, youth leaders and friends from small groups; those who have become significant to them.

If the church has emphasized a particular strategy or focus over the years, then candidates will most likely fit within your long-term strategy. When we recruit young people from our congregation, we have already spent years helping them to understand the difference between a healthy, focused and thriving agency and a mediocre agency. We have given them the tools, and the Lord has placed within their hearts a passion for specific types of ministry, like church planting, evangelism, discipleship, social justice or translation work. Over the years, our church leaders have invited speakers who have introduced the topics of unreached vs. reached people groups, community development, business as mission, and other ways of reaching people for Christ. Imagine the joy that comes as a result of training, encouraging, praying and then financially providing for young people who have been exposed to the world of mission, and now God is calling to His mission field.

WHEN A MISSIONARY DOES NOT FIT WITHIN THE VISION OF THE CHURCH

What if God has given someone another passion, affirmed by their gifting and experience, but it just does not fit within the strategic focus that you have worked so hard to establish? Here are a few options for your church to consider:

Option 1 — God may be stretching your church's vision to embrace them as an expansion to your current strategy. Otherwise, you are forcing them to find ministry partners from outside. It is not impossible, but it will take them much longer to build new relationships and acquire the partners necessary to sustain their ministry. Several missionary families in a particular agency carried the pain of exclusion by churches they loved which were unwilling to participate in the blessing of personal involvement with them in ministry. If at all possible, seek to develop your church's mission strategy so that people are first and projects are second. Training up tomorrow's missionaries should be a primary concern, taking into consideration that the mission field will definitely change over the long-term. Try to provide at least a nominal, perhaps even token support for those missionaries who grow up within the church. A small monthly gift will not impact a church budget substantially, and it gives the missionary an official place within the structure of the 'body'. If financial support is not possible, then make sure they have prayer, emotional and furlough support when they come home.

Option 2 — Seek to build partnerships with other local churches which may have an interest in the ministry to which the person has been called. If the church leadership takes an active role in connecting the missionary with another church that has a better fit for ministry, then your missionary candidate has developed a stronger support base. In the past, we have decided to be a secondary supporting church for a missionary who grew up here, but the primary sending church is in another city, and is clearly a better fit for what she has been called to do. We support her with a nominal amount every month, but we still pray and care for her, and she receives a great amount of support from the other church. For brevity's sake, we define a "Sending Church" as the one which takes full responsibility of a missionary on behalf of the agency for the purposes of Commissioning, Missionary Care, and overall development in partnership with the agency. Most agencies require a "sending" church before they will place a missionary on the field. A "Supporting Church" is a church that may provide funding, but does not "co-sign" for the missionary with the agency. The difference between a "sending" and a "supporting" church is not necessarily determined by the amount of financial support, but should primarily be determined by the closeness of the relationship.

Option 3 — Here is a recent example of creative and innovative thinking which allowed our church to grow in its understanding of how we interact with the global church, as well as the way we send missionaries to the field.

> **From All the World, to All the World**
> Jim and Sally feel called to go to Brazil to serve on staff for a campus ministry. Their home church has a very well defined strategic focus to do church planting among unreached Muslim groups. Brazil is not a nation known for its unreached Muslim people groups and doing campus ministry is far different from church planting. At first glance, there seems to be an impasse. However with careful thought and prayerful consideration, the Lord revealed to the church that Brazilian young people are being called in great numbers to the mission field, specifically to North Africa and the Middle East. There are many benefits for Brazilians to serve among Muslims: their lifestyle is more adaptable to these regions of the world, they are not viewed with as much suspicion as Americans, they are more cost effective, and they tend to be more enthusiastic as a culture. Jim and Sally are now working through a campus ministry to equip and empower these Brazilians to be church planters among Muslim people groups.

The global church is indeed changing and the role of the western church has a unique position from which to contribute. The church of the majority world is rapidly moving into leadership positions of organizations, agencies, and denominations. We no longer have the mentality of "from the west to the rest", meaning that the church in North America alone has the solution to the problems of the church in places like Sub-Saharan Africa. We no longer accept the mentality that we are the rich and powerful and they are the poor, so lets 'go and do' for them. Mission agencies are rejecting the flawed notion that western missionaries are the only people worthy of our support. Paul Borthwick recounts an experience at a Lausanne movement conference called *Singapore 87: A Conference of Younger Leaders*:

> "We heard phrases like 'the church going from everywhere to anywhere,' and 'the whole church takes the whole gospel to the whole world.'...We went to the conference expecting to hear how the church in North America was leading the global church into the new millennium. In contrast, we left the conference praying, 'Lord, please don't leave the church in North America behind as you move powerfully into the world.'" (Borthwick 2012, 14-15)

Certainly, there are more options available, but hopefully these three examples from our experience will help stimulate your thinking to pursue some sort of resolution for your current situation. We wrestle with the tension between wanting to be a church with a clear vision and a focused strategy, while at the same time honoring people as a priority over methods and models. After all, a church is about people not just programs.

WHEN A CHURCH ADOPTS A NEW VISION

What if the church adopts a new mission strategy which may no longer include a current missionary whom the church supports and the decision is made to no longer support this missionary? Within the parameters of *Mind the Gaps* model, this decision would not be made by the missionary care team. However, by minding the gaps, the care team can be an advocate on behalf of the missionary to the decision makers of the church. A compassionate response in the spirit of missionary care is to keep supporting him until his next furlough when he would be able to spend time seeking new partners.

These decisions grow more and more complex when we consider the role of the missionary care team. One of the benefits of serving on a care team is being in a non-evaluative role. Because of confidentiality, caregivers do not participate in discussions related to evaluating the performance of the missionary, therefore the missionary can confide without the risk of losing support. However, the downside is that the care team is not involved in the evaluation of the missionary's performance and does not know about downsizing until a decision has already been made. We have not found a perfect solution to this dilemma. There is a natural tension between the non-evaluative function of the missionary care team and decision making role of the Mission Committee. Somehow your church will need to decide on how communication will flow between the two teams with two seemingly opposing responsibilities. Given these tensions, we strongly believe that a separate care team is needed, apart from the Mission Committee, to value the person no longer being supported.

WHEN A MISSIONARY NEARS RETIREMENT

Unfortunately, some missionaries who are nearing retirement are sometimes removed from support by their church. This scenario is often a result of decreased networking since the missionary has been away from the church for many years. As a result, senior missionaries are often limited from developing new funding from churches because they are looking for younger missionaries to support. We personally knew a veteran missionary whose support was withdrawn because of a policy change by his sending church after 35 years of support. He was given one year while he was on the field to raise the additional support before funds would be discontinued. This was an incredibly difficult task. The decision makers were new to the church and did not know him well, nor were they familiar with his distinguished career. This could have been avoided if the church had an active missionary care team which helped to communicate his ministry on the field. However, he struggled the remaining eight years of ministry with inadequate funding because of the new policy. Missionaries are under a constant risk of losing support when there is a change in leadership of a church. Senior Pastors, Executive Pastors, Mission Pastors, Elder boards, Deacons and membership changes regularly, so developing a well defined transition strategy is very important for the missionary care team.

Again, a strategic focus for the church should consider people first and projects second. Some churches want to be trendy and try to imitate the church down the street. By taking the long view of missions and understanding that the mission field will look different in 15 years, or sooner, the church will be able to establish a long-term and viable strategic focus that will include the investment into future missionaries while valuing the contributions of retiring missionaries.

PARTNERING WITH MISSION AGENCIES

One final and very crucial aspect of choosing your missionaries is first vetting the agencies with which they will serve. On our website we have included our vetting procedure for your consideration as you develop your own policies and procedures. One organization that encourages fiscal responsibility of evangelical non-profit organizations is The Evangelical Council for Financial Accountability (ECFA). Membership in this organization can be a step toward greater financial credibility. You can have more confidence if the mission agency meets their seven standards of responsible stewardship required for membership. The ECFA encourages organizations to adopt these standards relating to financial accountability, fundraising and board governance.

The Evangelical Fellowship of Mission Agencies (EFMA) and Interdenominational Foreign Mission Association (IFMA) merged to form a new organization called Missio Nexus.

One of the functions of Missio Nexus is helping churches and mission agencies improve policies and standards of operation. A valuable article written by Marv Newell from Missio Nexus entitled, "Quality Standards for Agencies" is found in the Evangelical Missions Quarterly January, 2009 (Newell 2009, 94-98) and would be useful to any church vetting a mission organization.

For the purpose of clarity and to conclude this chapter, we want you to know we wrestled over the inclusion of this chapter. At first, it did not seem that the chapter fit within the context of a book addressing missionary care and emphasizing the importance of a non-evaluative, caring and nurturing relationship. However, in our experience, we have seen such a dramatic shift within mission oriented churches to have a very narrow and focused strategic vision for reaching out to a lost world. Missionaries are often caught in precarious situations, especially when they have multiple sources of support, all of which are looking for that illusive ROI (Return on Investment). They answer to the mission agency. They have to give account to their sending church. Their supporters want to feel like they are apart of the mission. In a perfect world, the economy grows at a steady rate and the church does not need to cut its budget. Heaven on earth would mean that people never lose their jobs, which allows them to continue supporting missionaries. And in this perfect world, the communication between the field and mission supporters is steady, regular and exciting. However, we do not live in a perfect world, and missionaries often feel excluded and left out. We hope that providing some perspective from our experience will help you and your church mind the gaps as you seek to be a witnesses for Christ in Jerusalem, Judea, Samaria and to the ends of the earth.

GET ON BOARD

1. Determine the strategic focus of your church. Start with the strengths of your missionaries and congregation.

2. If you want to broaden your focus, prayerfully consider a gradual plan to introduce it to the congregation. Use a slower approach than you may want, but one that will be accepted rather than rejected by the large group that changes slowly.

3. Prioritize a list of agencies you want to build a relationship with on behalf of your missionaries. Consider a manageable timeline and adjust your plan as necessary.

4. Identify the young people in your church who have displayed an interest in home or global missions. How might you encourage them? Guide their interest? Vet agencies that fit their gifting? Consider sending some of your young people to the next Urbana student mission conference.

5. When your pastoral and/or mission committee personnel change, determine how you will proactively introduce new staff to your missionaries and their ministries.

See MindTheGaps.org for more information on vetting mission agencies.

PART THREE

Making Connections

Developing Relationships

Introduction

David Wilson

With humility and repentance we confess, as a church, that we have ignored and neglected mission sending agencies as well as our own missionaries by the way we 'outsource' the Great Commission. We have participated in the sin of just putting a missionary's monthly check to the agency on auto pilot, placed their photo on the wall, said a prayer of commissioning and then went back to business as usual.

As time goes by, the church receives monthly newsletters, all with success stories to put in the file. However, they are often void of heartache or failures since missionaries are conditioned to believe that if they reveal a weakness, the church might withdraw their support. To compound potential issues on the field, I have observed that member care departments of many agencies are often over-tasked with ratios of up to 60:1 (missionaries: member care professionals), which prohibits them from providing individualized *proactive* care. They are often only able to be *reactive* when a problem arises.

Recently, I participated in a forum with a large sending agency which is trying to develop a stronger and more strategic connection with churches and their missionaries. The triangle relationship between the church, the agency and the missionary was evaluated, and we discussed how these three entities could form a more deliberate partnership. Among the many topics, participants agreed that the idea of church-based *proactive* missionary care could make a significant difference for missionaries on the field.

The following chapters should provide your team with tools, resources and ideas to cultivate the relationship between your church, the missionary and the agency. Regardless of size, your church can be highly developed when the care team considers the enormous potential in ordinary people. One of our core values in *Mind the Gaps* is promoting total congregational awareness and involvement in the ministry of caring for missionaries. The entire church should be intentional and fully invested in caring for its people who are sent out from among them.

When I ask missionaries, "What does missionary care look like for you?" the most common answer is simply that "someone sent me a note to let me know they are praying for me." Another frequent response is "my kids received a birthday package". Yet another response is "When I came home, people knew me and my work because they adopted me in their small group. They read my monthly newsletter as a group and pray for me every week." With all the complexities in the world of global mission, it is still the simple things that mean the most.

Without an intentional relationship structure in place, missionaries are often lost when they come back to visit their sending church. Because of transitions of staff and church leadership, they sometimes become unknown people who vaguely resemble that outdated ancillary photo on the wall with names that only come up during the annual budget meeting. They are not recognized nor do they feel honored as those who have been 'sent out from among us'. The next few chapters are intended to foster a thriving relationship between the principal partners involved in sending missionaries to the field: the missionary, the agency and the church. Establishing, cultivating and maintaining intentional relationships are vital to longevity and effective ministry on the field for our global workers.

Mind the Gaps is dedicated and committed to redeeming the past carelessness of the church and restoring its potential for global impact through its strategic relationship with missionaries and mission sending agencies.

Chapter 6

Connecting Through Prayer

Don Bell

"Prayer does not fit us for the greater work;
prayer is the greater work." — *Oswald Chambers*

> "We are so grateful for what the Missionary Prayer group represents to us. We know when urgent requests are given, they are going to be prayed for, that there is a group of people who know who we are and know what we're dealing with. When we come to visit, we aren't strangers, because they have been going through the journey with us in prayer."
> — *A Missionary from Trinity Church*

If, as James says, "the prayer of a righteous person has great power as it is working," (James 5:16) then it challenges us to consider how we can pray effectively for missionaries. We will look at both praying as a form of care and praying for their work to be successful, because these are both bound up together and cannot be separated.

Before we jump in and look at how to mind the gaps and pray effectively for missionaries, we should remind ourselves why we pray. We pray because there are spiritual battles that must be fought with spiritual weapons. Ephesians 6:12-13 says, "For our struggle is not against flesh and blood, but against the rulers, against the authorities, against the powers of this dark world and against the spiritual forces of evil in the heavenly realms." In the very early church when the apostles first took on the responsibility of leading the newly birthed Christian Church, they identified two overriding priorities for their personal attention, their job description as it were: Prayer and the ministry of the word (Acts 6:4). If prayer was a top priority for the Apostles in the first century, there is every reason why it should be just as high a priority for us in the twenty first century. This is of strategic and spiritual importance. We invest heavily in financial and training resources for our missionaries to ensure their success, and we need to invest equally in prayer.

PAUL THE MISSIONARY ON PRAYER

As a missionary himself, the Apostle Paul provides some instruction on how the churches were to pray for him and for others doing the work of the gospel. Here are a few passages where Paul solicits prayers from his friends and supporters:

> *I urge you, brothers, by our Lord Jesus Christ and by the love of the Spirit, to join me in my struggle by praying to God for me.* (Romans 15:30)
>
> *Devote yourselves to prayer, being watchful and thankful. And pray for us, too, that God may open a door for our message, so that we may proclaim the mystery of Christ, for which I am in chains. Pray that I may proclaim it clearly, as I should.* (Colossians 4:2-4)
>
> *Finally, brothers, pray for us that the message of the Lord may spread rapidly and be honored, just as it was with you. And pray that we may be delivered from wicked and evil men, for not everyone has faith.* (2 Thessalonians 3:1-2)
>
> *Pray also for me, that whenever I open my mouth, words may be given me so that I will fearlessly make known the mystery of the gospel.* (Ephesians 6:19)

Paul says that through prayers, others can join with him in his work. His prayers also reflect his pastoral concern for his readers. Our missionaries are children of God first and missionaries second, so all of the pastoral concerns we see expressed in Paul's prayers are completely appropriate for our missionaries today. It is very easy to focus our prayers on practical requests and problems that need immediate solutions, but we want to include the spiritual issues of the inner person as well. Here are some of the pastoral prayers from Paul that are meant to encourage his readers.

> *With this in mind, we constantly pray for you, that our God may count you worthy of his calling, and that by his power he may fulfill every good purpose of yours and every act prompted by your faith. We pray this so that the name of our Lord Jesus may be glorified in you, and you in him, according to the grace of our God and the Lord Jesus Christ.* (2 Thessalonians 1:11-12)
>
> *I pray that you may be active in sharing your faith, so that you will have a full understanding of every good thing we have in Christ.* (Philemon 6)

Your missionaries need to know you are praying for them and what you are asking the Lord to do. That is a sincere form of encouragement and a much appreciated reason to let them know they are not forgotten. Here are some additional prayer items for you to bring before the Lord as you pray for your missionaries:

- They would know the hope to which God has called them, the riches of His glorious inheritance, and His incomparably great power
- God may strengthen them with power through his Spirit in their inner being
- To grasp how wide and long and high and deep is the love of Christ
- To know God's love that surpasses knowledge
- They fall deeper in love with Jesus, the lover of their soul
- They be filled to the measure of all the fullness of God
- To be filled with the knowledge of God's will through all wisdom and understanding

- Their love may abound more and more in knowledge and depth of insight, so that they may be able to discern what is best and may be pure and blameless
- To be filled with the fruit of righteousness
- By His power He may fulfill every good purpose and every act prompted by their faith
- The name of our Lord Jesus may be glorified in them
- They may be active in sharing their faith
- They keep their eyes on Jesus and not their circumstances

KNOW YOUR MISSIONARY

These are general things from the scriptures about praying that can be applied to any and every missionary, but part of offering up effective prayers for missionaries is praying for the specific issues they face. Not all missionaries are the same. They are in different stages of life, live in widely different places geographically, socially and culturally. They have a great variety of ministries and face different challenges.

A strong missionary care team will take the time to really know their missionaries. They will make opportunities to spend time with them, attend presentations they give on their work, engage them in conversation, take them out to lunch, discover their heart for ministry, understand their vision and listen to their concerns. Caregivers will form a relationship with couples and families as individuals. Different members of a family will have different perspectives, different vision and different challenges and anxieties. Learn about the context in which they live and serve. Learn about the kind of ministry they have and their ministry goals. Missionaries will share things they would like prayer for in their newsletters but as you get to know them and really listen to them you will see things to pray for that they don't explicitly mention. When they do share specific needs, respect their requests and pray for them right away. These are things which are of great concern to them and they are looking to God for help.

PRAYING WITH OTHERS

Be faithful at remembering to pray for your missionaries by following Paul's example. There is also something to be said for praying with others who share the same concerns for missions and missionaries. In Matthew 18:19-20, Jesus said, "If two of you on earth agree about anything you ask for, it will be done for you by my Father in heaven. For where two or three come together in my name, there am I with them." Praying with others can provide accountability, mutual encouragement and opportunities to learn more about the missionaries and their work. Scripture gives principals to apply to your missionary prayer groups:

> *Though one may be overpowered, two can defend themselves. A cord of three strands is not quickly broken.* (Ecclesiastes 4:12)
>
> *As iron sharpens iron, so one man sharpens another.* (Proverbs 27:17)

An added benefit of missionary prayer groups, in terms of missionary care, is that having a group will foster more personal involvement and connection with missionaries. It is also a great encouragement to missionaries on the field when they know that there is a group back home who are minding the gaps and praying for them. When they return to their supporting churches, they know there will be a group who knows about their work and life and has understanding of what they are doing.

A faithful missionary prayer group will strengthen any church's mission program, but a word of caution: missionary prayer groups are only truly effective if they actually pray. There can be a strong temptation to either spend most of the time just talking about the prayer requests or just socializing among the group. Prayer groups must be diligent and disciplined to do the spiritual work to which they are called.

HOW TO PRAY

Below you will find suggested topics to help stimulate your prayers for missionaries. This is not an exhaustive list, but over the years we have experienced a wealth of insights into the real needs of missionaries through prayer. Sometimes we receive a prayer request for one thing, but there is an unsaid prayer which exists apart from the email. Through developing an intimate relationship with our missionaries, we are often able to see the underlying issues with which the missionary is concerned. There are also times when the missionary goes 'underground' and we do not hear from them for a period of time for a variety of reasons. During those dark and uncertain times, the prayer team needs some guidance about what to pray. Our hope is that this list will help make your prayer time more productive and beneficial.

Relationship with God

- Pray that the missionary would continue to grow in their own relationship with God: Growing in love, faith and knowledge, becoming conformed to the image of His Son.
- Pray that they would experience His joy and peace, and that the fruit of the Spirit would be manifested in their lives.
- Pray for sensitivity towards the Spirit's leading.
- Pray for perseverance when times are discouraging, and that they would not grow weary in doing good.
- Pray that they stand firm against temptation and not compromise their moral integrity.
- Pray for confidence in their call and pray that God would protect their hearts from envy towards those with a different call. (Those that answer the call to missions often find a certain amount of sacrifice which comes with the call.)
- Pray that they would not neglect their own prayer life or neglect time in scripture.
- Pray for spiritual refreshment and nourishment. (Some missionaries serve where there is limited or no opportunity to

experience corporate worship and they may not have the benefit of pastors and teachers building into their lives.)

Relationship with Others

- Pray for strong marriages and close friends.
- Pray for their spouses and children, and that each member of their family would prosper. (Many missionary families have to leave the field sooner than they had expected because a child was not prospering.)
- Pray for love and unity among teammates. (Conflict among team members is sometimes a great source of stress and can be the cause for a missionary to return home prematurely.)
- Pray for the missionary's relationship with those in authority over them in their work.
- Pray for their relationship with national workers and church authorities.
- Pray for their relationships with extended family and supporters, whom they may not see for years at a time.
- Pray that God would give them a love for the local people and that the barriers of language and culture would be overcome.
- Pray for an attitude of forgiveness. (Opportunities to be offended and wronged abound on the mission field.)
- Pray that love would rule all their relationships.

Their Specific Work

- Pray for opportunities for the gospel to be presented and that God would lead them to those hearts He has been preparing.
- Pray for people to come to Christ and grow in their faith.
- Pray that God's church would be established.
- Pray that the church plant would be a faithful witness to the community.
- Pray for godly leaders to be raised up to serve.
- Pray for men and women who will be faithful to take on the responsibility of teaching and discipling others.

- Pray that God would give them words they need when they have opportunities to speak.
- Pray that the missionary be diligent about fulfilling their specific responsibilities.
- Pray that they would not depend on their own abilities but that they would depend on the power of God at work in them.
- Pray for national helpers to come along beside them and help with the work.
- Pray for new missionary teammates and for additional teams to join them in the broader work.

Ask the Lord of the harvest, therefore, to send out workers into his harvest field. (Matthew 9:38)

Wisdom

- Pray that God would give them the wisdom they need (missionaries face very challenging situations, sometimes with little structure to guide them). James 1:5 gives us confidence that God will hear and answer this prayer. "If any of you lacks wisdom, let him ask God, who gives generously to all without reproach, and it will be given him."
- Wisdom on how to partner with locals and how to entrust work to nationals.
- Wisdom for what strategies to pursue.
- Wisdom on how to use their time, what tasks to take on and when to say no.
- Wisdom on how to encourage and challenge disciples, and how to equip them for service.
- Wisdom on how to interact with governing authorities.
- Wisdom on how to live so that their reputation is not undermined among those to whom they minister, their ministry partners, and among those who send them.
- Wisdom in dealing with conflict of any kind.
- Wisdom on how to be a blessing without fostering dependency among those they serve.

- Wisdom for those in closed countries on how to represent themselves and how to conduct themselves and their work so as not to endanger themselves or others.

Practical Issues

- Pray for spiritual protection from the forces of evil and from evil men.
- Pray for protection from disease. (Some live in areas where protection from disease and sickness is a very real issue.)
- Pray as well for physical protection from religious and political enemies. Pray for changed hearts for those who oppose them.
- Pray for favor from governing authorities.
- Pray for language acquisition and the ability to communicate well in an unfamiliar language. (Our ability with a language can affect how people perceive us.) Pray for ears to hear and tongues to speak unfamiliar sounds. Pray that missionaries who are in language study would invest the time needed to learn the language well and be free of distractions.
- Pray for friends, but also pray for the ability to cope with loneliness.
- Pray for the ability to figure out how to adapt and "do" life effectively on the field. (In some places in the world, the actual work of daily life can just be hard and take more time than we are used to in the west.)
- Pray for trusted national friends who can help navigate unfamiliar cultural practices. (Living in another culture can be challenging, bewildering and emotionally draining.)
- Pray for faithful financial supporters. (Failing financial support is a stressful burden for missionaries to bear.)
- Pray for new supporters who share their vision and would welcome becoming a part of their support team.

[*As of the writing of this book, our missionary prayer group has been meeting every Sunday morning for the last 18 years. The author of this chapter and the leader of this group, Don Bell, has been faithfully leading prayer and connecting our congregation to the needs of missionaries by receiving timely requests, sorting them onto a prayer list and making sure that people pray for the missionaries. Our missionaries have complete assurance that there is a faithful group of people who will present their names to the Lord every week. When they come to town, this is the first group they go to see, like a wonderful family reunion. Creating a missionary prayer group is the first priority that must be done. There is everything to gain from having an intentional time of focused prayer for those whom you have sent out from among you. There will be much cause for rejoicing when you hear answered prayers from the mission field. — Editor*]

GET ON BOARD

1. Initiate a regular prayer group that will faithfully pray for your missionaries. Choose someone to lead the prayer effort.

2. Begin contacting your missionaries weekly asking for prayer needs as well as answers to prayer they have experienced.

3. Include prayer for the spiritual needs as well as the practical needs. Use some of the suggestions in this chapter to actively incorporate this important aspect of prayer. You are welcome to use any of the suggestions under "How to Pray."

4. Use Skype or similar technology to speak with your missionaries during your prayer time. When they are in the area, include your missionaries in the prayer group.

Chapter 7

Connecting the Missionary to the Care Team

Paula Lawrence and Linda Parker

Paula's Story

When we made our new home overseas, it took a whole year to grieve the loss of the blessed friendships and tender care my Trinity Church family had provided. There were multiple sendoffs and prayer meetings and a strong sense that we were an extension of those we left behind. They would be with us every step of the way.

In that first year in our host country, I was aware of a strong intentionality to meet people, and the adrenalin of those newly purposed early months tempered that loss even though there were times of real loneliness. Within two or three years, friendships in my host culture began to grow and replace friendships at home. It seemed to me a healthy turnover of relationships, but it just wasn't possible to maintain the same level of relationships with those we left behind. I accepted that gap while on the field.

Coming home though was a different story. I found it a huge challenge to communicate with people about what our life has been like the last three years. How can you sum it all up in three minutes on stage on a Sunday morning? The breezy "how are you?" and "I'm fine," left me wondering at times if people had the ability or desire to really understand what our lives were like. When someone said, "Oh, I could never do that," I wanted to quip back, "Hey, if I could do it, you could!" It was a weird feeling, too, when some supporters who gave of their finances while we were away didn't really want to meet with us when we were at home.

> Then there were those who really wanted to listen that made home feel like home again. In our case, it was a faithful group on Sunday morning that communicated with us and prayed for us while we were away. They were so glad to hear about what God did, and how we, and our kids were doing, personally. It made reconnecting so much easier.

Connect — to join or fasten together, to become united, to consider as related, to establish a rapport or relationship with (www.thefreedictionary.com). As you can see from the title of this section, making connections is one of the primary goals of our missionary care team. We did not want our missionaries to feel disconnected with their home church. We started as a team to build relationships with our missionaries since we were going to serve as a link for them to connect with others in the church.

CONNECTING WHILE AWAY

Each missionary and his family is assigned to one of the members of our care team so that we have the time to really get to know three or four of them, utilizing already existing relationships as much as possible.

This is an area for our care team to really make a difference. We want our missionaries to be able to step back into their church lives as seamlessly as possible. With the help of email, Skype, and worldwide instant message applications, every member of our care team considers developing relationships with assigned missionaries to be their central responsibility. The desire is to connect monthly and keep abreast of any prayer requests and needs. In the initial communication, we introduce ourselves as the liaison from the care team, their "go to" person in the church, but as time passes, we hope to develop a mutual friendship, if one does not already exist. Any needs they have at home or on the field can be communicated to the rest of the team at our meetings. It proves difficult in some cases to keep this regular contact, but our monthly meetings help with the accountability for this. Our desire is to share in these meetings any updated prayer requests and to brainstorm how to meet needs presented.

The missionary's level of need and desire for personal contact can vary greatly. Some may appreciate more frequent interaction and find it a lifeline. Others may be so busy that it could become bothersome or they may have many significant relationships to keep contact with already. Each situation needs to be handled individually, but overall we have found this regular contact to bring safety so that the missionary can be more vulnerable to share needs.

CONNECTING WHILE AT HOME

What better way to connect as a care team when missionaries visit than to sit and enjoy a meal in a home together? We provide a home-cooked dinner and create a relaxed time of sharing when we know our missionaries are in the area. During this time we remind them of our purpose as a team and our desire to care for their needs whether large or small, but most of all, we allow time for them to just talk. The missionary is used to reporting on their ministries to committees, supporters and staff, in sometimes very brief periods of time. We set the stage, up-front, that this time is different. We want to create space with an understanding of confidentiality, and found issues have surfaced that they may be facing on the field, questions surrounding their church involvement arise, or they discuss personal issues in which they want prayer.

Plan on the unexpected when it comes to providential moments as sharing occurs. These are times when the care team finds itself in the center of critical moments in the life of the missionary. In this sense, a gap of care appears right before us. One such time happened with our team as the missionaries were in the midst of making very difficult decisions regarding a family member. The sweetness of sharing, crying, praying and providing some counsel was a burden-bearing blessing for everyone there. They were not alone and knew others cared and loved them through the difficult time. Too often, these burdens are carried silently by the missionaries, because of the concern for judgment or evaluation which can bring financial ramifications. Sharing with those who will have a deeper level of understanding and praying for issues such as their heart's need for a marriage partner, marriage issues, financial struggles or balance in their already overcrowded schedule can be a great comfort to the heart of the missionary.

On our website (MindTheGaps.org) you'll find the Care Plan Interview Form that can be used as a guide when making regular contact with missionaries while away or at home. After (not during) our meetings with them, we fill out this form, bring it to our next meeting, and use it to plan together how to meet needs that came up in our communication with them.

The assigned care team member is also responsible for caring for a spectrum of the missionaries needs when they are in the area. This happens best by finding out what they will need during that time regarding housing, transportation, meals, medical help, babysitting, etc. We have developed a Resource List of people from the congregation that have volunteered to help with these needs (see chapter 12, Practical Needs). Rather than just handing the list to our missionaries or posting it on our website, we ask that they contact their care team liaison who will make sure that a volunteer is able to fill that particular need.

CONNECTING THROUGH A FIELD VISIT

Want to have your eyes opened? Visit your missionaries on the field. This has been a wonderful way to build an understanding bridge of care and love with our missionaries. On our visits we sometimes minister alongside the missionary in their endeavors, bring tools such as communication skills training which they can use in their ministry or provide counseling or assessment services for children's needs. If they have time, we like to take them away for one or two days to a place of natural beauty nearby for spiritual renewal. And of course, taking care of the children so mom and dad can spend some alone time together is a much-appreciated service. Just as important, is creating space for precious times of sharing in their homes and ministries in their cars, around their tables, with their foods and their friends on their soil. A field visit goes a long way to connect your hearts and build trusting relationships that show them how important they are to us. The visit opens up vistas into the challenges these tough soldiers are facing day to day for our Lord and we see it as critical to bridge the understanding and compassion gaps that can so easily exist with the miles, time and differences in a foreign country. Our eventual goal on this team is that each team member visit the missionary they are assigned to on the field.

CONNECTING AT A RETREAT

One additional vision the Lord has given our team to care for our missionaries has been a yearly retreat for those who take the time and expense to come off the field to attend our annual missions conference. It's our gift to them during a busy week of speaking and meeting people, just to get away for a day or two of rest, interaction with each other, fun activities and input that would nourish their souls. Included are pertinent topics to missionary life such as conflict resolution tools, soul care material, as well as times in scriptures with our pastors. Our missionaries especially appreciate the opportunity to share with others who understand missionary life. The retreat actually becomes a strong motivation for some of our missionaries to be willing to come home for the conference, knowing that it will be a time of restoration for them. We keep the cost low by using homes provided by our congregants, keeping with our core value that our local body minister to our missionaries.

God designs relationships to do the work of His kingdom. Soon, the strong relationships you build will create a link in the chain of caring that flows from the care team, through the church, to the missionary.

GET ON BOARD

1. Pray, then brainstorm with your team, about ways the Lord may be leading you to develop relationships with your missionaries.

2. What would you like to do to connect with your missionaries while they're away or at home?

3. How will you find out about their needs, and how do you plan to meet those needs?

4. Look at your Philosophy of Ministry and incorporate the core values that apply. Decide what goals will help the care ceam develop these relationships and the specific ways (methods) that would accomplish these goals.

Chapter 8

Connecting Missionaries to the Congregation

Donna Stark and Joan Morrill

Squeals of Delight

"I really wish you could have heard the squeals when that box was unpacked. What a thoughtful treat from our small group!" This, from one of our missionary families in Europe, was music to our ears indeed. The small group that had adopted this missionary family had a wonderful time shopping and packing a shoe box for the missionaries' three children; a box from America filled with stickers, coloring books in English and more. You can bet that missionary couple did not feel forgotten by their home church as they watched their children open that box.

Forgotten. It's a word that too often describes how missionaries may begin to feel as they are living far from their home of origin. When they first leave for the field, it is often with a wonderful commissioning and send-off with the prayers of people who know them, love them and appreciate what they're doing. But as the years go by and the busyness of life overtakes those in the home church, memories can fade and good intentions of staying in touch can fall by the wayside. Another factor is that churches change. Pastors and staff leave and are replaced by new staff who don't know the missionary personally. Members move away and new members come who also don't know the missionary.

The sad result is that there are those on the field who never hear personally from anyone in their home church and who can identify with that word *forgotten.* A missionary we know who had served for three years in China was at her home church, ran into a church member she knew and was asked, “Oh, I haven’t seen you for a while. Have you been on vacation?” I’m sure they laughed after the missionary answered that they had been in China for three years, but it was also probably embarrassing for the church member and a bit sad for the missionary.

As parents, our missionaries are extremely concerned about their children. They know their children did not choose to live in a foreign land or have to learn another language and culture. Therefore, anything that we can do to make the children of our missionaries feel loved will minister to the parents.

STRENGTHENING CONNECTIONS

So how can we help strengthen connections between the members of a church and the missionary family? Here are a few ways we attempt to do that:

- Each week in the worship folder a different missionary is featured. Their picture is included along with current information about their ministry.
- During that week at our women’s Bible studies, that same picture is shown on the screen and in the opening prayer someone prays specifically for them.
- A display is set up each Sunday with pictures and information about our missionaries.
- A bulletin board is posted in the department where children see it. We learned from a questionnaire some of their favorite things and some of the differences between our country and their new country. Many of the adults who pass through these halls also enjoy learning about our missionaries.
- We send a “Birthday in a Box” to all our missionary kids. One of our missionary moms had told us that one thing her kids missed was an American birthday party. Using the questionnaire as a basis, we described our TCK (Third Culture Kids, aka Missionary Kids or MK) including their birthday,

age and items of interest. At various venues, we challenged people to take these information sheets and prepare a birthday shoebox for their TCK filled with anything they could squeeze into the box, keeping it to two pounds for reasonable mailing costs. Through the positive response and feedback we've received from both parents and kids we discovered that when we do something for the TCKs, the parents feel loved as well.

- Each summer our church has a one-week day camp activity with lots of electives for kids from kindergarten to sixth grade. We decided to have a class based on the countries where we have missionary kids. We chose five countries, one for each day of camp. Then we sent an email to the missionary parents asking them to describe interesting customs in their country. To make the experience authentic we made imitation passports with a stamp that said MISSION DEPARTMENT, with our church name, city and ADMITTED on the Visa. Each day we stamped the country they were visiting. We discussed each country, showed its flag, gave a quiz, shared a special food, played a native game and made a craft.
- We initiate regular correspondence with our TCKs from our church kids twice a year. We match ages and give the church kids information about the TCKs and then ask them to write a note or, in some cases, to draw a picture.
- When missionaries come home, they are often introduced in the worship services, either on stage or by just having them stand and be acknowledged from their seats.
- At 8:00 a.m. each Sunday, people gather to pray specifically for our missionaries. Our leader provides an updated list of prayer requests and we pray through this list. Many times, one of our missionaries passing through Redlands comes to this group and gives us current updates on their lives and ministry. Invariably, they tell us how very much it means to them to know this group faithfully prays for them.

HIGHLIGHTING THEIR MINISTRIES

Our annual Mission Celebration Week is a time when we focus on missions in general and on our missionaries in particular. During this week those missionaries who are able to come:

- Visit different small groups to share about their ministries
- Introduced at an international dinner
- Usually given an opportunity to set up a ministry display
- Speak in various classes (both children and adults)
- Featured at an evening service

Many congregants go home with a colorful placemat of all our missionaries' pictures. It is a beautiful collection and hangs somewhere in the homes of many of our members as a year-round reminder to pray and communicate with our missionaries.

ADOPTING THEM INTO SMALL GROUPS

Another important component of our effort to connect our missionaries to our congregation is our small group adoption program. A little history on how this program began for us may be helpful. Several years ago some of us attended a missionary care conference and heard some great ideas. But the one that especially resonated with us was the idea of having each of our missionaries connected to at least one small group in the church that would support them in prayer and keep in touch. They were called Advocacy Groups at the conference and it was suggested that for each missionary, we pull together people they knew to form their own Advocacy Group.

We returned home enthusiastic and began to talk to people about joining a missionary's Advocacy Group. However, we ran into several obstacles; the biggest one being people's time (or, to be more accurate, the lack of it). In order to be a true Advocacy Group, it seemed that the group would need to meet, at least periodically. The problem? People are busy, and adding one more group meeting to their schedule just wasn't an option for many. As a result our optimism dimmed and we shelved our project for a while. The project was a little daunting for us as well. With almost 30 missionary units, if there were only five people in each Advocacy Group, that was about 150 people we would need to recruit and organize.

But, thankfully, today each of our missionaries has a small group that has adopted them. So how did this happen? It happened when we made the decision to dispense with the idea of forming a new group but instead used the church's existing small groups. Like many churches, we have a ministry of small groups meeting in homes during the week. For us, this was truly the more natural avenue for the group-missionary partnership. Each of our missionaries has at least one of these small groups that has adopted them and claims them as their own. And it has been a delight to see the groups support their missionary.

The key to making this happen is to present your proposal to the church's small groups/education leader and work with him. But keep in mind that because the church's small groups are often asked to do a number of things, asking them to adopt a missionary can sound a little overwhelming. That's why we came up with a list of only five things we ask them to do. They are not time-consuming, but they also leave room for creativity and more involvement if the group wants to do more. We wanted our small group leaders to know that this was not a big commitment time-wise.

Here are things we include on each newsletter that is sent out to the small group leaders:

Take Five!

How to support your adopted missionary

1. Pray for your missionary weekly in your prayer time.
2. Send them a picture of your small group.
3. When they are at Trinity include them in your group time.

4. Communicate with them monthly. This can be one person or a 'taking turns' set-up. It can be a phone call, email, letter, birthday card, video, package, etc.
5. Anything else you care to do. Use your creativity!

To begin the process of matching groups with missionaries, we were given the opportunity to come to a small group leaders meeting and explain the adoption idea. From there different groups requested certain missionaries because someone in their group knew the missionary personally. This is a great connection, but not necessary. Other groups asked that we just assign them one. Before we knew it, all of our 23 missionaries were assigned a group.

To help them begin we gave each group the "Take Five" list and information about their specific missionary. This included a picture, their mailing address and email address, birthdays, and a little about their ministry. For missionaries serving in closed countries, the group must also be given important information about using caution in their communications with those missionaries. We also suggested that they ask the missionary to add interested group members to their prayer letter list. That way, the leaders aren't the only ones keeping up with their prayer requests and ministry.

If you are planning to start a missionary adoption effort in your church, you should also know that starting it is just the first step. Maintaining it is the key to its being an ongoing support. You've heard the phrase "life happens." Well, that is true in this endeavor as well. Group leaders change, groups disband, they get busy and forget their missionary, missionaries are added and they leave the ministry, and the list continues. Ongoing maintenance is vital.

One thing we do is to phone through our list of adoptive small groups each fall to see if they are still a group and if they are still keeping their missionary. If a group has disbanded, we find a replacement group. Another good ongoing connection is to send out newsletters that highlight what certain groups have done for their missionary and to express appreciation for all the groups. It's not only fun to see others' ideas, but it's motivating and a good reminder.

The amount of involvement varies widely from group to group. Most groups do a good job and are a great blessing to their missionary. Some, however, get busy and tend to forget. The important thing to remember is that even though it's not a perfect program, it greatly increases the personal involvement of your congregation members with your missionaries and is well worth the effort.

JOINING WITH THEM IN MINISTRY

Like many churches, we send our members on short-term mission trips. As much as possible, we try to send these groups to the places where our missionaries actually serve. As you might imagine, this is where people really discover the real stories from the life of the missionaries and their ministries. When you're eating, traveling and serving together, it is a great partnership and time of bonding.

A Means to an End

A missionary couple in France had identified a community with a population over 100,000 which had no evangelical church. They found a facility to rent which could be used for a church, but lacked the means to do an effective outreach. They wanted to provide value to the community and become acquainted with some of the families in the neighborhood. Their sending church had an especially gifted group of musicians in the college ministry along with a heart to minister to people for the cause of Christ. The church sent these young people to do a music camp for the children in that city for two weeks during the summer. At the end of the second week, they invited the community to a production in their rented facility which exhibited what the children had learned during the camp. This gave the missionaries and other Christians in the neighborhood a time to meet and form a relationship with each other. The team helped to demonstrate care for the children and their families which eventually led to the planting of a new church.

In Paul's letter to the Philippian believers, he makes clear to them that their prayers and involvement with his missionary travels strengthen and encourage him greatly. “I thank my God every time I remember you. In all my prayers for all of you, I always pray with joy because of your partnership in the gospel.” (Philippians 1:3-5) Our prayer is that our missionaries feel strengthened and encouraged, knowing that they are remembered in prayer and that we are truly partners with them in the furtherance of the gospel.

GET ON BOARD

1. How does your church involve its people in the lives of your missionaries?

2. Specifically, how are the missionary children included in the life of the church?

3. Review the bullet points throughout this chapter and relate the ideas listed to the programs of your church.

4. Begin to form a strategy unique to your church, to pray and partner with your missionaries to ensure that each family is known and loved by caring individuals and groups within the congregation.

Chapter 9

Connecting with the Sending Agency

Bill & Betty Jane Born and David Wilson

New Missionary Candidates

"We chose this mission agency because we sincerely believe it will care for us as members," one missionary told us.

As the candidate committee for a sending agency met with each proposed missionary, one question that was asked stands out in particular. "Why do you want to be a member of this agency?" This is a good and thought provoking question that some candidates had already thought about and others, surprisingly, entertained for the first time. Although this is a good question to ask, the answers provided by these potential missionaries are far more important.

We were on the agency staff and were invited to be a part of the orientation. Families, married adults and singles from all walks of life were coming because they desired to serve the Lord on the mission field with this organization. Some were quite young, others more experienced with life and raising a family. Each had the desire to serve the Lord of their lives; the Christ who had brought them His salvation. Every individual came with a photograph etched in their mind of what he/she was going to do if accepted into the agency. That photo was particularly important to each one and it had gotten them this far — all the way to becoming a missionary candidate.

Some stated that they knew someone already in the agency. Others liked what they had seen in recruitment videos or brochures and some had read about it in the missions media. A few were missionary kids familiar with the organization while growing up on the field. But the overwhelming reason given for wanting to serve the Lord through this agency was because of its reputation of missionary care.

As a church care team, one of the most caring things you can do for prospective missionaries is to help guide them to agencies with a reputation for care and a willingness to work alongside the church to make the missionary's career successful. So, what are some of the fundamental areas within the agency you should look for? Here are some perspectives for your team to consider.

SENDER CARE (ALSO CALLED EMPLOYER CARE)

How do you mind the gaps and help your missionary choose an agency that really cares? Both the missionary and the care team should consider this valuable question to assist in the success of their missionary. It has been said, "You can tell many things about a person when you look at their calendar and their bank account." The same is true for mission agencies. Do they have staffing which reflects an emphasis on care? Do they offer member care retreats? What about health care, retirement options, and personnel field visits?

Kelly O'Donnell says that sending agencies "...demonstrate (their) commitment by the way they invest themselves and their resources, including finances, into staff care. Sending groups aspire to have a comprehensive, culturally relevant, and sustainable approach to member care, including a commitment to organizational development. Sending groups do well to offer quality services **for** staff and to expect quality service **from** staff." (O'Donnell, 2002, 18)

The church-based missionary care team should help candidates discover their selected agency's stated purpose of caring for their missionary. How does the sending agency indicate they will value and care for new staff? It may be helpful to look at this particular area using the concept of Employer Care. Employer Care can also refer to the legal requirements of the mission organization. This is vast in both breadth and dimension and in some mission circles this particular area of resources is called Sender Care. As you consider both the local and state laws applicable to the sending agency, consider the dignity of the individuals from Christ's perspective which requires that you operate from a higher level. Does care include being proactive, or is it just reactive? Is there a focus on prevention to reduce the times intervention is necessary? An allocation of resources, both human and financial, is required in order to carry out a good program of caring for each member and to be able to implement affirmative, loving and truth-filled care. This signals the value and importance that a mission agency places on caring for their staff. Here is a list of what encompasses agency member care which your church team should carefully evaluate. Not all of the items on the following list will exist but this should be a starting point for consideration by the missionary care team. This list will also help the care team identify some of the gaps of care which the agency does not meet so your care team can be effective and offer complementary assistance:

Personal Standards

- Retirement provision: financial and situational planning
- Financial planning: tools for stewardship with a vision of good financial practices
- Vacation and holiday guidelines: proper rest and recreation
- Managing personal expectations: misunderstood and missed expectations along with conflict resolution training
- Spiritual growth and development: good practices to sustain their faith and trust in the One whom they serve

Legal Standards

- Salary requirements and guidelines: both legal and moral salary requirements that will enable the appointee to be effective
- Governing labor laws: meeting requirements of local, state and national government labor laws
- Social Security requirements: future retirement and medical care
- Workman's compensation: accident and injury needs while on the job

Health, Safety and Security Standards

- Health care: wellness care and health issues may include but not be limited to hospital in-patient and out-patient, doctor visits, laboratory needs, dental prevention and restoration, medications, emergency medical needs both domestic and foreign
- Personal safety and security issues: to include both on-the-job safety as well as plans for safety in times of crises—civil, political and natural disasters
- Emergency contingency planning: crisis management and ministry coverage

Educational, Training and Development Standards

- Training and Preparation for Field Service: Training or the lack thereof directly effects missionary success.
- Continuing Education: This has a direct impact on the longevity of workers. It reduces stagnation, values the missionary, and produces intellectual growth.
- Missionary Kid Education: Available choices include, but not limited to boarding school, local schooling, national online schools, and home schooling.
- Re-Entry: Returning to the home culture can be more difficult than culture shock, so preparation and instruction must be given to reduce reverse culture shock.

Ask your missionary for a copy of the mission agency's personnel manual or handbook.

This is a helpful resource for you to use and compare from one agency to another. On our website (MindTheGaps.org) you will find our agency questionnaire that we give to our missionary candidates. We ask our missionaries to do their homework and find out for themselves what the agency offers. Then we have them report their findings back to us. This has been very helpful for us in determining if we, as a church, can agree to support the agency or not. The agency and the church needs to be aligned with one another so that a relationship can be formed and cultivated. Through this relationship, the care team has the potential of identifying gaps of care for their missionary.

> **A Veteran Missionary**
>
> Years ago, Martha left the United States to serve the Lord. She was a great missionary. Many opened their hearts to receive the Good News and countless individuals turned to the Lord as a result of her service for over 40 years. As time and years took their toll, she returned to her homeland because her health was failing and her energy had diminished. Martha went to her home church and asked if they could help her after all these years.
>
> To the surprise of church leaders, her sending agency had never prepared for this eventual time in Martha's life—no health-care plan, no financial plan, no retirement plan. Essentially, the responsibility now fell to her church to care for her. Thankfully, the church rearranged their budget and individuals from the congregation stepped forward to assist her in practical ways.

In contrast to the veteran who never thought of salary, health-care, or retirement benefits, things have certainly changed. Today, new recruits ask direct questions of agencies regarding the benefit policies they provide for their families and their futures. It is no longer uncommon for a recruit to ask about the items listed above in the 'employer care' or 'sending agency care' categories. Such items have become a priority, even a necessity, for most sending agencies. Is it wrong for recruits to ask up front? Does their question imply a lack of trust in the Lord's provision? Is it 'unspiritual' as Martha may have concluded years ago? As a care team, your understanding of these significant issues prompts appropriate questions to sending agencies on behalf of both the veterans already on your roles as well as the new candidates you are considering. With first-hand information of the benefit packages available to your missionaries, you can influence the quality of their care and effectiveness because you are fully aware of how their agency cares for them.

CLARIFYING THE ROLES OF THE AGENCY AND THE SENDING CHURCH

A definition for a "Sending Church" can be the one which takes full responsibility of a missionary on behalf of the agency for the purposes of Commissioning, Missionary Care, and overall development in partnership with the agency. Most agencies require a sending church before they will place a missionary on the field. On the other hand a "Supporting Church" is a church that may provide funding, but does not co-sign for the missionary with the agency. The difference between a "sending" and a "supporting" church is not necessarily determined by the amount of financial support, but primarily determined by the closeness of the relationship.

The sending church and the sending agency each desire to increase the effectiveness of their missionaries by caring, praying and financial giving. The agency invests a very significant amount of time, energy and resources to prepare and send a missionary who will be effective. Since both want the same positive results, they must work together towards that end. As a church care team who is minding potential gaps, it is most important that you maintain contact with the sending agency's member care department and develop a personal relationship with their care team representatives. Seek out those with whom you can freely communicate and work together to find ways to demonstrate the highest level of care for the missionary. Obtain name(s) and contact information so that there will be good communication right from the start. We made the decision that someone from our care team would personally visit the headquarters for all of the mission sending agencies with whom we partner. This has been a very enjoyable exercise for our team and a rewarding use of our time.

The church and agency have unique contributions to the care of the missionary on the field. At Trinity Church, we have discovered a slight, but profound difference that may help you begin to understand the need for both church and agency involvement in the lives of missionaries.

A Tale of Two Missionaries

Two missionaries were sent to serve with the same agency, from the same church, to the same country of Central Africa. Allen and Mike went to serve the church there through an agency that provided very little pre-field cross-cultural adaptation and interpersonal skills training. After only a few months, a conflict developed between Mike and Allen which required intervention by the member care staff at the agency. Since the conflict had progressed to a point of being irreconcilable, the agency had to make a decision to remove Mike from the field and bring him back home to the U.S.A. They made this decision for the sake of the mission and not necessarily for the sake of the missionary. Mike came back to his home church as a wounded missionary who was sent home from the field. The church was now in a precarious position of providing care for both Allen who was still on the field and Mike who had been sent home. The agency had freed itself of caring for Mike so that their mission could continue.

Because of this situation, Trinity Church discovered a very specific frame of reference for our contribution to missionary care. Though not true of many agencies, this agency made its work on the field their priority. Meanwhile, our church made its priority the care of the person. This distinction can only be discovered in these types of extreme cases. The church needs to understand its role of caring for the individual while at the same time understand that the agency has much larger issues on the field to consider for the success of kingdom work.

Under normal operating circumstances, the church and the agency can pair together and share resources without necessarily dividing up roles and responsibilities. Some agencies will have a broader and more widely developed care program than others. That is why it is important for the church to take a good inventory of services provided by each of their agencies represented. The gaps in care from one agency to another can be identified, and then a customized care plan can be developed for each of the missionaries based on the understanding of what each agency provides. Emphasis must be placed on proactive and preventative care, and then provide reactive and intervention types of care when needed.

There will be times when the church care team has the ability to fulfill a need that the mission agency cannot fill. That is what we call a "gap in care," and this can only be discovered by an intentional group of individuals within the church who are tasked with the role of developing relationships with both the missionary and the agency. A well established relationship will most likely be very helpful to the agency and appreciated by the missionary. Such events can be routine and some are in times of emergency. If there are medical or emotional emergencies, the missionary will most likely want to be near family or their home church.

> **An Emergency**
> While a little boy's parents were taking a break at the local pool from the rigors of language study, a missionary child in pre-school almost drowned. The lifeguard's rescue was quick, but sadly brain damage was permanent. After immediate help was administered locally, their mission had funds set aside for emergencies and flew the family back to the U.S.A. for prolonged treatment to improve the child's motor and cognitive skills. The home church immediately offered to locate housing, transportation, and the best professionals to treat the child. Everything was in order when the family arrived. The church filled gaps which the agency could not possibly perform.

The home church is a great asset when it stands ready at any moment to help. The church is generally capable of doing more than the agency with the wealth of resources available within a congregation, which can be mobilized to help in specific situations.

> **The Newlywed Compromise**
> A young newly married missionary couple approached their church for support. Their agency had given them the green light to begin raising support for their mission. As the time came closer for the couple to leave for the field, the agency called the church with awkward news. During their orientation, some relationship struggles emerged due to multi-cultural issues in their marriage. The agency

> thought it was best to postpone the couple's departure. The church did not agree with this assessment and was very eager to have a new missionary on the field. A compromise was reached that the couple would delay their departure for a year. The church agreed to help this couple go to marriage counseling, attend a couples retreat and discuss a few books together with other married couples. This turned out to be a very beneficial solution; one in which the church and the agency could celebrate the successful launch of a promising couple onto the mission field.

When a church and agency work closely together, there is the potential for disagreement between the two entities. Difficult circumstances will arise involving who should make a decision. Questions such as, Who has the authority and the final say? What is the role of the church in this situation? Since the church gives financial support, doesn't that mean it gets to make the final decision? Brazilians have a saying, "He who pays for the band is in charge of the party." These can be tough questions with difficult answers. Yet, the solutions generally exist when humility, honest dialogue and open hearts are mixed with a previously established relationship. A church may believe their contribution to the missionary's support gives them the control over the missionary, but it's not the proper way to look at this relationship.

The church and the sending agency both desire effectiveness and longevity for the missionary. We see this relationship in much the same way as a dance. There is give and take, push and pull, lead and submit, but if done with grace and humility it can be a very beautiful thing. The church should communicate well and make sure that all perspectives are on the table, but keep in mind that only one can be in the lead position. In general, the sending agency has the final authority over the one who was sent out. It is the sending agency that has accepted, trained and sent the missionary under its umbrella of protection. They have carefully selected the individual or family because they believed they would work well within the purpose of the agency. There are also legal concerns which the sending entity must adhere to regarding local, state and national requirements for visas, benefits and other employment regulations. They assign the missionary where they have ministry needs, and they work with them on a daily basis. They play the valuable role of doing all that is necessary to make the missionary effective in the kingdom of God.

However, we have discovered some exceptions to this general rule. In researching for this chapter, we interviewed various mission agencies and asked the question, "In a difficult circumstance, when various parties are in disagreement, who makes the final decision?" There were several agencies, with whom we have a relationship, which gave different answers. One organization said that the church has the final authority. From their perspective, the church should be in the lead role and the agency was providing a service to the church. This agency has a very high view of the church and is intentional about developing a relationship with church leaders. They offer a Church Partner Forum twice a year, and invite church leaders to come to their sending base for a three day orientation whenever they have a new missionary candidate. Another agency delegates their authority to the field leadership. Once a missionary is placed on the field, their team leader is given the last word in any disagreement. Yet another agency responded that the missionary has the authority to call the shots. With such a wide variety of responses, we have concluded that it is best to ask the question "Who has final authority?" for each missionary on your list. Better yet, write up a Memorandum of Understanding (MOU) between all parties involved and keep it on file. As the years go by, leadership changes, policies change, and relationships change, so a MOU will help resolve issues in the worst case scenario. Remember that a healthy, intentional and vibrant relationship between all parties is the key for successful missionary support.

From our perspective, the church's role is to come alongside the agency with the same goals in mind, but with the desire and capacity to mind the gaps. The church may know the missionary far better than the agency since he/she likely grew up in the congregation, gave his/her life to the Lord, were discipled and heard the call to mission service in the church. However, sometimes the church has blind spots which keep them from clearly evaluating their missionary. There may be an emotional attachment or an over zealous desire to send people out to represent the church on the mission field. On the other hand, with thoughtful evaluation, the church is in a great position to provide specialized personal care, because of their intimate knowledge of the family/individual.

> **"I Feel Like a Failure"**
> A church missionary care team went to visit a single woman missionary working in a sports ministry under the supervision of a local pastor in an isolated town in SE Asia. While there, the missionary frequently made comments that led the team to believe that there was an inappropriate relationship developing between her and one of the young men in her church. She was certainly very lonely and felt isolated from people her own age. Her immediate supervisor was from another country and there were no other missionaries in her agency in this region for many miles. The missionary care team contacted the agency immediately after their visit and gave them a report of their suspicions. Unfortunately, the agency did not follow up with a field visit. They only had a video chat from the supervisor. Despite the urging of the church based care team, the agency refused to do anything about the situation. Out of frustration, and a variety of other reasons, the church decided to withdraw support from this missionary in an effort to bring her back to the U.S.A. The agency disregarded the church and continued to support the missionary for another nine months until the inappropriate relationship with a particular young man was fully revealed along with a pregnancy, pictures, and outrage by parents in the local church.

The church and the agency need to build a mutually respectful relationship that is more than just a passing check and donation receipt in the mail. At Trinity Church, we are beginning a five year plan to grow closer to only a few agencies with whom we are compatible, so that we can partner more deeply. Some agencies are beginning to develop strategic partnerships with churches, and in turn, churches are seeing mission agencies as more than just an entity for 'outsourcing' missionary candidates. For reference, here are some of the things we want to see in an agency. This is not a comprehensive list, nor do we feel this is what every church should look for in an agency. This is the list we put together to help you get started. Tailor your list to suit the needs of your church:

Team based — We have not seen many consistently good results from independent and self-determining missionaries who are on their own out in the field. The team is our preferred model since it has built-in accountability and some valuable emotional and security benefits.

Field led — The agencies which are on the cutting edge and see the best results are often those who are not 'top-down' leadership; but they are field driven. There are a few agencies which have frustrated their missionaries by making decisions that seemed right in one context, but did not work in another context.

Member care — This is a relatively new concept in the mission world when you consider the totality of the world Christian movement since the days of William Carey and Hudson Taylor. As you form a personal relationship with the member care representatives, ask questions like:

- What is the ratio of missionaries to member care personnel?
- Is there a separation of evaluation and missionary care?
- Does the agency provide retreats, seminars, and other proactive care?
- Is there a plan for regular visits and team building?

Training/mentorship — Some agencies offer field orientation, cultural adaptation, language acquisition, and other pre-field training. Others offer outsourced training through groups like CIT (Center for Intercultural Training) in North Carolina and MTI (Mission Training International) in Colorado. There are pros and cons for both methods. Our only requirement is that missionary candidates participate in some form of training that is relevant to their particular place of service and method of ministry. We are active in evaluating a missionary candidate's needs from the very beginning.

Oversight — Just as we form a personal relationship with the member care representative for our missionary's agency, we also form a relationship with their direct field supervisor. We make sure that there is someone who has accountability for them. We want to know what their contingency plans are in case of emergency, so that if they experience problems on the field, we will know how to be proactive in the help we can provide without getting in the way of mission leadership. Our goal is to be a blessing and not a burden to the work being done on the field.

When the missionary care team of a church joins with the mission agency, there is a powerful synergy that takes place which results in an effective, happy and healthy missionary on the field who is serving the kingdom of God in amazing ways.

GET ON BOARD

1. What does the missionary photo look like that is etched in your candidate's mind?

2. Why did the candidate choose their agency?

3. Collect and study the Personnel Handbook from all the agencies with whom you partner.

4. Connect with the mission agencies and begin to develop relationships with the member care personnel and with your missionary's direct supervisor.

5. Brainstorm with your team to discover what your church would like a missionary sending agency to provide. Then, mind the gaps.

PART FOUR

On the Journey

Meeting Needs

Introduction

David Wilson

This book would be endless if we just looked at the needs of our missionaries, so let's focus instead on God's provision and the calling which He has on your particular church to care for missionaries.

One day, while visiting South Africa, I asked the pastor of our partner church, "How do you decide who to help? You are surrounded on all sides by a vast sea of needs. No church could help everyone with all of their problems, and yet you are making a deep impact into your community. How do you determine who gets what?" With typical African wisdom that comes from a wealth of experience, he referred me to God's original design at creation. "David," he said, "when God created the world, was it not filled with everything that man would need?" I answered, "Yes, scripture says that the world was 'filled' and it was 'good.'" "At what point did man begin to have a need?" he continued. "When sin entered," I replied. "And who was responsible for bringing sin into the world and creating such a need?" My response was a perplexed half answer, half question. "Satan?" The conclusion from my friend was, "If God is the creator of provision and plenty, and Satan is the creator of need, then why should we focus on the needs, when we should be looking at our provision? When we focus on the provisions which God has placed before us, then we can decipher God's calling for us to be a conduit of His blessing and supply. If we completely focus on the needs around us, then we will tire and burnout because it never ends. But God is a god of plenty and His supply will never expire."

That was the day that Matthew 6 finally made sense to me in the grander scheme of things. The song "Seek Ye First" is a beloved memory from my early years after surrendering my life to Christ. But how could it apply to the complexities of leading a church in the expansion of the global missionary enterprise?

Frankly, there are times when I catch myself so entrenched in the needs of people, whom I am called to care for as a shepherd, that

I forget to "seek first the kingdom of God and His righteousness..." This verse is not a command, but a promise. It is more of (borrowing a computer programming term here) a conditional statement: "If/then." The last part of the verse is important when we consider the needs of people, "and all these things will be added to you." My personal paraphrase of this verse now is: "IF you seek first the kingdom of God and His righteousness, THEN all these things will be added to you."

A church should not ignore the needs of its people, but do not let them become the driving force for your team. The work you will be engaged in with missionaries is spiritual and God ordained, and He cares for His workers far more than you do. I assure you that if you seek the Lord's provision first, He will guide you every step of the way. He knows what your missionaries need and he is already making the provisions for your church to be the answer to their prayers before they are prayed. Your primary task is to remain connected to the Lord and sensitive to His Spirit's leading. Even now, He has provided your church with leaders and care givers to form a missionary care team. "Ask and it will be given to you; seek and you will find; knock, and it will be open to you." (Matthew 7:7)

Chapter 10

Spiritual Needs

David Wilson

> "Humble yourselves, therefore, under the mighty hand of God so that at the proper time he may exalt you, casting all your anxieties on him, because he cares for you. Be sober-minded; be watchful. Your adversary the devil prowls around like a roaring lion, seeking someone to devour. Resist him, firm in your faith, knowing that the same kinds of suffering are being experienced by your brotherhood throughout the world. And after you have suffered a little while, the God of all grace, who has called you to his eternal glory in Christ, will himself restore, confirm, strengthen, and establish you. To him be the dominion forever and ever, Amen." (I Peter 5:6-11)

For those serving in the role of pastor to missionaries, let's consider four aspects of your ministry to them: The Spiritual Battle, Spiritual Disciplines, Spiritual Endurance during Hardship, and Spiritual Qualities for Resilience.

THE SPIRITUAL BATTLE

Missionaries are called by God to be the ones who remove the prey from the mouth of a prowling, ravenous, roaring lion. Our enemy, Satan, is described in scripture as one who roams 'to and fro on the earth' (Job 1:7 & 2:2), seeking to harm, discredit and separate people from God's divine plan to prosper, restore and redeem mankind (Jeremiah 29:11-14). Throughout scripture, we are made painfully aware that our battle is "not against flesh and blood, but against spiritual forces" (Ephesians 6:12). This spiritual battle is present in the life of every believer, but missionaries put themselves in harm's way intentionally just by answering the call of God to "go therefore and make disciples of all nations" (Matthew 28:19). This calling goes against the wishes of a ferocious, yet clever enemy.

Our missionaries are engaged in a spiritual work for the Lord, so we must realize that only Almighty God is capable of meeting the spiritual needs of missionaries, not the church, the mission sending agency, friends, family members, co-workers, and even pastors. As senders, we are called to walk alongside our missionaries to be encouragers, mentors and supporters, but not as a replacement for God's Holy Spirit.

In II Chronicles 20:15, King Jehoshaphat receives a message from the Lord saying, "Do not be afraid and do not be dismayed at this great horde, for the battle is not yours but God's." Preceding this powerful declaration of God's faithfulness is a humble admission of weakness and humility from the king, "For we are powerless against this great horde that is coming against us. We do not know what to do, but our eyes are on you" (verse 12).

The wisdom comes from that last sentence, knowing that the battle is not ours, but God's. This is His work and we are called to serve alongside Him. King Jehoshaphat's words still apply today. While we live in a world of instant communication with access to quick information, our international partners often find themselves saying, "We just do not know what to do." In ministry, a common temptation is trying to minister in our own strength, but may our prayer always be that our missionaries keep their eyes on Jesus, the author and perfector of our faith (Hebrews 12:2).

SPIRITUAL DISCIPLINES

God, *Through Her,* Helped Me Grow

Sue went through a very dry period spiritually while in Indonesia. One day, she was speaking with another missionary and being very

> open and honest with her. "Is this all there is?" she asked. Neither of them were having consistent time in the scriptures. They were just going through the motions and it seemed as if there was no life in their relationship with God. Putting it simply, they were bored. So they decided to hold each other accountable spiritually and asked God to meet with them daily. They met for Bible study and for prayer five days a week. That was a period of great spiritual growth in Sue's life. With that accountability, they were able to watch God come alive in scripture together. And not only that, they held each other accountable in other areas like weight loss, relationships with their husbands and children and other goals the Lord placed on their hearts.

During missionary care conferences, you will often hear about the need for missionaries to have strong habits in the spiritual disciplines. These habits need to be strong in order keep their relationship with Christ vibrant, since they may not have the frequent access to spiritual input as in their home country. We sometimes use these disciplines as a discussion guide to gauge the spiritual temperature of a missionary, especially when they are showing signs of burnout. We ask what elements are missing in their current practice and how they can be reintroduced into their normal routine.

One excellent resource to help caregivers think through the spiritual disciplines is Richard Foster's *Celebration of Discipline* (1978). He writes from the Quaker tradition and skillfully categorizes spiritual disciplines, which are helpful in understanding the spiritual life and needs of every believer:

- Inward Disciplines:
  Prayer, Fasting, Meditation and Study
- Outward Disciplines:
  Simplicity, Solitude, Submission and Service
- Corporate Disciplines:
  Confession, Worship, Guidance and Celebration

SPIRITUAL ENDURANCE DURING HARDSHIP

One of the chapters in *Tender Care* (Wilson and Kronbach, 2010), has given us incredible clarity as we wrestle with the idea of meeting the spiritual needs of missionaries. Collaboratively written by missionary caregivers at Barnabas International, it is a practical guide filled with wisdom and insight gained through experience. The title of the chapter is "A Necessary Theology of Suffering." They summarize by saying:

> "God has designed the human soul to require hardship as a major ingredient for maturity. Thus, the care provider's primary responsibility is to work with God as He works in and through other's lives and ministries in the midst of victories and afflictions. We serve God and His servants well when we increase our understanding of God's use of affliction in the shaping of our lives and develop the capacity of our hearts to journey with others in those hard times." (Tender Care, p.165)

There is a difference between common knowledge and the biblical mandate for commandment keeping. Common knowledge says, 'If someone strikes you, then you should get even.' Commandment keeping says, 'Turn to them the other cheek' (Matthew 5:39). Common knowledge says, 'We should not send good people into dangerous places in the world.' However, the commandment in Matthew 28:19 says, 'Go into all the world.' Common knowledge says, 'If you are suffering hardship or pain, then you should avoid the source.' Commandment keeping says, 'Share in suffering for the gospel by the power of God' (2 Timothy 1:8). Well-meaning and good-hearted Christians can sometimes get in the way of what God is trying to do in a missionary's life. Christians are often prone to accepting the norms of their own culture and society, while ignoring some very basic and fundamental principles from scripture. Western Christians are notorious for seeking comfort and security since they are surrounded by these luxuries at home, but when they leave for the mission field, they need a new set of skills and abilities in order to survive the rigors of life outside of their comfort zone.

The Apostle Paul understood that a vibrant spirit comes through the rigorous exercise of faith. Much like the muscles in our body require exercise to keep from atrophy, our spirit needs to be trained through spiritual exercise, which is often very uncomfortable. We often try to make things easy for the missionary, while thwarting significant life lessons which they need in order to survive a harsh life on the mission field.

> "The human soul needs difficulty to reach maturity, just as physical growth often involves stress, challenge, or pain." (Trauma and Resilience, *Schaefer and Schaefer,* 2012, p. 4*)*

Anyone who has trained for an endurance sport, like a marathon or triathlon, knows that the training is difficult, laborious and fraught with unseen risks. Reading a fitness manual, discussing the workout methods with a trainer, or watching exercise videos are only the beginning of the physical development. The athlete needs to experience the training on the road and in the elements in order to build up stamina for the race.

The Endurance Race

Recently, my wife and I (David) trained for a race. We started slow and gradually built up our endurance by challenging each other to go further and faster. There were a few times when I noticed that my wife was having difficulties, and I began to experiment with helping her build confidence. I knew that her muscles were capable, but with endurance sports, the brain is the most important part to condition. At times I would encourage her by saying "We are almost there, keep going." At other times, I would challenge her by saying "lengthen your stride, breathe deeper and let's go a little faster" which helped her break stride and stretch a little. Another time, I prayed for her. My prayer was not that God would take away the pain or hardship, but that she would endure through the pain and embrace the hardship, knowing that this exercise was making her leaner, stronger and more confident.

Our missionaries need a challenge to build up their spiritual muscles. When we pray for our global workers who are working in difficult places, it is *nice* to pray for safety, but it is *better* to pray for them to be good stewards of their lives. Jesus prayed for deliverance from the cross, but he also added, "Nevertheless, not my will, but yours, be done." (Matthew 26:39-42; Mark 14:36; Luke 22:42)

When our workers send a prayer request asking for intercession for a hardship they are experiencing, it is *nice* to pray for the hardship to be removed, but it is *better* to pray for endurance through the hardship. Romans 5:3-5 teaches us that "suffering produces endurance, and endurance produces character, and character produces hope, and hope does not put us to shame, because God's love has been poured into our hearts through the Holy Spirit who has been given to us."

One of the best prayers for missionaries is that they would experience God's presence. We often hear people express prayers that go something like this: "Lord, be with our missionary during this time." However, Jesus said in Matthew 28:20, "Lo, I am with you always" and the writer of Hebrews 13:5 quotes the Lord in saying, "I will never leave you nor forsake you." Therefore, a biblically inspired prayer would be more like, "Father, help our missionary to be constantly aware of Your presence as she goes through this trial. Give insight into what You are doing in and through this situation. Give confidence, not in herself or her circumstance, but in You and Your everlasting care and provision for every need."

SPIRITUAL QUALITIES FOR RESILIENCE

Those with experience in missionary care often observe certain spiritual characteristics that evidence a connectedness to their Lord which sustain them spiritually while on the field. Karen Carr of the Mobile Member Care Team in West Africa identifies certain qualities: (*Schaefer & Schaefer,* 2013, p. 93-95).

1 — Knowing One's Call

The call of God comes to different people in different ways. Sometimes the call is initiated by a spouse. Others are more dramatic such as the specific calls which Bill Bright and Billy Graham received as young men when Henrietta Mears challenged them and others at a Christian conference. The scriptures are full of call experiences, so there are plenty of ways in which the Lord has communicated to his appointees.

However you may define "calling," the research is clear, that having a clear sense that God has called you and the church has confirmed that call, is the strongest factor in preventing missionary attrition. (*Worth Keeping*, 2009, p. 93-95) So, how do you determine the genuineness of that call in your missionary candidates? Each church is different, so take some time to discuss with pastors and missionaries from your context to determine what "calling" looks like in your church environment.

2 — Utilizing Praise, Gratitude and Joy

Missionaries who are able to utilize praise, gratitude and joy in their everyday lives, and especially in difficult times can only do so supernaturally as a result of deeply knowing the unblemished character of God. A personal theology of suffering enables the missionary to praise God and give thanks because the deep questions produced by suffering promote an abiding faith in God and an empathetic love for others.

3 — Grace Rather than Performance

Built into the missionary experience are expectations, whether real or imagined, that come from being carefully chosen, trained, and financed to represent Christ in another culture. It is a high honor with high hopes attached to it. Most missionary training centers, because of this natural human tendency to produce results and the western concept or performance necessity, build into their training module a healthy understanding of one's brokenness and how to minister out of weakness.

Broken and Ready to Go

During a missionary training course the trainer pointed out a missionary candidate who was taking the course a second time. He said, "We didn't allow him to go to the mission field after the first time he went through the course because he didn't know he was broken. He knows that now, and he's ready to go." There has been a healthy shift in missionary training over the last ten years toward helping missionaries accept their brokenness. Because of this, they recognize God's grace so they can minister out of God's power rather than their own strength.

Pastors and missionaries need to learn how to minister out of God's power and not just rely on their own skills and abilities. In *Trauma and Resilience: A Handbook* (2012, p. 95-98) there is an excellent description of what can go awry in a missionary's spiritual walk.

4 — Being Able to Forgive

Offenses will come, and there are certainly many opportunities for hurt on the mission field, both from inside the organization and from external sources. Sometimes new missionaries are marginalized because they have not yet "served their time," as some of the older missionaries on the team may say. A team member may have the need to "fix" another team member. There is hurt when nationals betray our workers by stealing or spreading rumors. There may also be times when the agency leadership makes decisions that negatively affect them.

Being able to forgive is both a personality trait and a spiritual discipline. Some people are raised with a strong sense of justice, which can interfere with one's ability to forgive in a case where justice is denied. Some of our missionaries have been sheltered from hurtful situations during their lives because they were raised in Christian homes. We praise God for strong Christ-honoring families, but in an over-protected environment, they may not know what to do with offenses when they come, because they have not had the opportunity to develop that spiritual muscle of forgiveness.

A TASK FOR THE WHOLE CHURCH

Where do missionaries learn how to fight spiritual battles, cultivate spiritual disciplines, develop spiritual endurance in hardship and acquire character qualities for resilience? Does the mission agency have the time to cultivate these qualities in their candidates? Hardly, but they can and should screen out those applicants who don't have them. Should we send some who have the passion to go, but lack some of these qualities, believing that they will grow into them on the mission field? After all, aren't we all in process? Perhaps, but we must consider the cost to the global church.

Make every effort to see that your church is God's instrument to build these disciplines and qualities into the lives of its future missionaries from a young age, and encourage them in your current missionaries. Churches should be intentional about building these qualities from childhood through adulthood in its teaching, mentoring, and modeling.

Many agencies foster the spiritual growth of missionaries in a number of ways. They may have spiritual retreats. Some have member care personnel who will visit workers on the field to encourage them spiritually. Most regularly chat via online video calls. And still others provide resources like books, teaching videos, and online training designed to encourage spiritual growth and discipline.

One of our missionary couples experienced a very dry time spiritually. As a result, they moved into missionary care for their agency, providing spiritual retreats to missionaries from their agency who may have had similar experiences. They know first hand the importance of ensuring the spiritual vitality of field workers who can feel cut off from the rest of the world.

What is the role of the missionary care team in the local church? How can we come alongside the agency and help? What are the gaps of care as we address the spiritual needs of a missionary? We see the spiritual lives of our missionaries as so foundational that they deserve another set of eyes to see, ears to hear and hands to help in this crucial area. Here are some ways we do that at Trinity Church:

1 — Relationships

Build trusting relationships that yield honest answers. If we did the hard work of building relationships of trust, the simple question, "How are you doing spiritually?" can yield honest answers that open the door for coaching and prayer with them.

2 — Intercession

Stand with them in prayer for the spiritual battle. Self-doubt is a common trait among many missionaries. Satan is the accuser of the brethren (Rev. 12:10) and he may use their work or even past sin, to make them doubt they are worthy or capable for the task. When there seems to be no real basis for the self-doubt, we simply acknowledge Satan's attempts to discourage and stand with them in prayer.

3 — Accountability

Ask them about their spiritual habits. As our missionaries leave for the field, we ask them, "How do you plan to feed yourself spiritually?" Benjamin Franklin once said, "If you fail to plan, you are planning to fail." If missionaries have a plan in place, then they will be more likely to succeed especially if they are going to an unengaged and/or unreached people group where there is no viable church to stimulate spiritual growth.

4 — Retreat

Provide a relaxed forum for vulnerable sharing. Our care team uses our annual retreat with missionaries to help them look at deeper areas of the heart. Here are some things we do with them in a peaceful and undisturbed setting:

> **Confession** — Confession is good for the soul. One of the tools we've found to be helpful is *Determining Your Idols.* Idols are things we all have learned from our families or culture to rely on for our wellbeing other than Christ, such as achievement, safety, respect or approval from others, and control. (See MindTheGaps.org for a reflective tool called

Determining your Idols). In this retreat setting, confession of faults and sins to one another naturally takes place, which leads to prayer and repentance.

Accountability — We've also taught about having an accountability partner with whom they can share vulnerably and give permission to "speak into their lives" regarding areas that could trip them up spiritually. This may help keep them on track with a spiritual habit.

Forgiveness — We assume that missionaries, just like us, have the need to forgive others and to be forgiven. So when we meet with our missionaries in a relaxed setting, like a retreat, it is helpful to talk about hurts they've experienced and how to walk through these with forgiveness. They can share their struggles and victories in forgiving, find a common experience of mutual caring, and pray for one another as they seek healing.

CONCLUSION

At some point in our development as a western church, we have embraced the gods of safety and security. Our lifestyles have influenced the church more than scripture. As a result, we send missionaries who have not developed a theology of suffering nor have they built up spiritual muscles to endure hardship, which they will encounter on the field. This is leading to increased attrition. Missionaries need a church that fully invests in their spiritual vitality and is training them to keep their eyes fixed on the Lord in all circumstances. Our global workers are in harm's way and they have an enemy who will exploit every spiritual weakness they may have. Their only hope in times of trouble is the Lord, so the main priority for the local church is to lead them to develop spiritual muscles that will enable them to thrive on the mission field. In a psalm of hope for the coming Messiah, the Psalmist cries out to God, "Save me from the mouth of the Lion" (Psalm 22:21).

GET ON BOARD

1. **Building relationships of trust.** Discuss with your missionary care team whether your relationships with your missionaries have the kind of trust that will give them the freedom to answer honestly when asked the question, "How are you doing spiritually?" If not, how can that trust be built?

2. **Spiritual battles and spiritual habits.** How do you stand with them in the spiritual battles they face and encourage them to maintain good spiritual habits? How important do you see accountability relationships as a way to maintain spiritual health? Look at the reflective tool, *Determining Your Idols,* on our website for your own spiritual growth. How could this, or other tools you are familiar with be used in the lives of your missionaries to increase the normalcy of vulnerability and confession within the community of believers?

3. **Endurance during hardship.** In what ways can you lead those considering missionary work to develop a personal theology of suffering? Consider this is not easily done through simple teaching, but also through grappling together with truths in small groups where transparent sharing can take place. Perhaps this process will enable you as a caregiver to wrestle with the questions that your missionaries may ask.

4. **Certainty of one's call.** Discuss with your pastoral leadership what constitutes a person's call from the Lord to missionary work. What importance do you give this in choosing missionary candidates and how do you affirm or verify that call? What are ways in which you as a church give opportunities for your young people to realize a call to minister in another culture?

5. **Living in praise, gratitude and joy.** How well do you, as a caregiver live in praise, gratitude and joy as you go through life's

difficulties? What in your life helped cultivate that? How is your church cultivating this in its members and future missionaries?

6. **Grace rather than performance.** Besides Biblical teaching on salvation by grace, how does your church encourage its members to live in God's grace rather than perform for others' or God's approval? What do you look for in your missionary candidate that gives evidence of this? How can you identify and help those who don't realize or accept their brokenness and are ministering out of their own strength?

7. **Living in forgiveness.** What successes and challenges have you had personally with forgiveness? Does your church encourage its members to live in forgiveness? How can you cultivate forgiveness as a lifestyle in future missionaries?

Chapter 11

Emotional Needs

William Britt and Linda Parker

> "Even in our emotionally taxing world, Christians can enjoy the best of emotional health." (Tim Clinton, editor, *The Soulcare Bible,* page 1041)

Have you ever asked missionaries about heart-rending experiences they have had? Missionaries experience emotional pain: pain in leaving family, friends and familiar culture behind, and pain in problems on the field like team conflict, family issues, and the stress of intercultural adjustment. At times, there is the pain of their own lack of effectiveness, and pain if they give into temptation, like most of us. There is sometimes pain in trauma that the missionary experiences, such as war, death of a loved one, assault or robbery. In fact, statistics gathered by the Mobile Member Care Team serving 14 West African countries show that missionaries experience significantly more trauma than those at home.

> In West Africa, 92% of the male and 85% of the female missionaries reported one or more severe traumas in their life. In Europe, 82% of male and 73% of female missionaries reported one or more severe traumas. In comparison, in a sample of the general population of the U.S., 61% of men and 51% of women reported one or more severe traumas. The differences are even greater when comparing these three populations by who had experienced three or more severe traumas. (Schaefer and Schaefer, 2013).

Even more eye opening is a breakdown of types of severe trauma experienced by West African missionaries while on the field.

> The most common traumas for the West Africa missionaries were serious illness (61%); car, train, or plane accidents (56%); unexpected death of family member or close friend (51%); immediate exposure to fighting, civil unrest, or war (48%); burglary (41%); serious threat or harm to family member or close friend (38%); seeing another person seriously injured or dying as a result of accident or violence (34%); and evacuation (31%) (Schaefer and Schaefer, 2013).

Christians with a heart for missions who look at statistics like these will surely see the need to help missionaries with emotional pain that inevitably results from such experiences lest we underestimate the enemy's ability to neutralize God's global workers in this way. However, church caregivers may have two responses to a chapter like this. They may feel compelled to hand this job to professional counselors due to feeling inadequate in the face of such difficulties. And, some are leery that we are attempting to put church missionary caregivers into the role of counselors. On the contrary, the church has a unique role in this area, and we invite you to consider some gaps in care that we can and should fill.

As you encounter the emotional needs of the missionary, here are some questions you might ask. What is normal to the experience of the missionary, and how can you be an encouragement to them through it? How do you know when things have gone beyond normal adjustment difficulties, team conflict or typical family struggles so that you may step in and find the missionary outside help? How does Christ meet our missionaries in their emotional pain? How do you walk with them during a crisis to support their recovery?

These are some of the questions we hope to address in this chapter. We will do that in two ways. Where our own experience is helpful, we will include that. And where other people have done an excellent job at addressing a particular issue, we will give a review of their material for further reading.

When Normal Hardships Arrive, They Can Handle It

On short term trips to visit our missionaries I (Linda) almost always came away with an appreciation of their willingness to move through some of the hardships of living interculturally with God's grace and wisdom. Initially, with my profession as a counselor I would be unduly concerned for their emotional well-being. Some of the things that would disturb us at home are just normal aches and pains to our missionaries. They appreciate our trust in them to go through these things while remaining strong, with the Lord's help. Though watchful, I trust God more that life on the field won't bring them down emotionally. And, after having been with these people, I have to stifle the temptation to tell my clients back home, "Stop your bellyaching!"

One of the things we as the care team have found is that our missionaries really appreciate it when they can tell us some of the emotional pain they're feeling due to cultural or team adjustment, loneliness, and self doubt. They must be assured we trust them to have the strength to deal with it rather than attribute their pain to "dysfunction" in their lives. With a policy of confidentiality in place, the church caregiver is in a unique position to be a sounding board and vehicle for prayer for some of these normal aches and pains without worry as to how that will affect their financial support. Many times just being a fellow pilgrim, who with them, can carry the burden to God for His strength is enough. Jonathan acted as this burden bearer for David when he was discouraged: "And Saul's son Jonathan went to David at Horesh and helped him find strength in God." (I Sam. 23:16, NIV)

It's All Okay

A few years ago, at a member care symposium, I (William) learned about different stages a missionary team will go through as they develop into a cohesive, effective group. During one of these stages there may be considerable turmoil as team members' expectations are discovered, negotiated, renegotiated, and finally resolved into norms of how to interact. This may take up to two years. Knowing this I will have a better response to our missionaries who are going through team struggles, and can be a sounding board when they need it without being afraid that where they were sent is just not working out. Instead of the church prematurely rescuing them by bringing them home, we on the care team can remind them that this is the normal process of team development, and God will enable them to give grace during their difficult times as a team (Tuckman, 1965).

FOUR STAGES OF TEAM DEVELOPMENT

- **Forming stage:** This is the "honeymoon" of team life. All is new and abstract for the team members' vision, relationships and field environment. The team has yet to be tested, and if this formation period fails to go well, the next stage, "Storming" will be even more difficult. These stages are in dynamic tension; each time new people come into the team, the process begins again, and different team members may be at different stages.
- **Storming stage:** During this time of testing and turmoil, the team learns how to complement their commitment to the work God has called them to with trusting relationships. Cross-cultural stress, coupled with being in a small intensive community, may cause the team to harbor a dislike of the culture, the team, and the leader.
- **Norming stage**: Group cohesion and a sense of normality develops; members accept the team and norms are developed for conflict resolution, decision-making, and goal completion.
- **Performing stage:** Relationships, structure and purpose have been cemented and the team can now effectively work toward the task (Tuckman, 1965).

NORMAL LOSSES OF LIVING INTERCULTURALLY

Also, a part of normal adjustment is certain losses missionaries might experience as they move into another culture. With every change, losses occur. The care team can help remind them that they are not unspiritual or losing their minds, but are experiencing the normal losses that occur when so much must be given up that is familiar and sustains their identity. L.A. Dodds and L. E. Dodds (Member Care symposium 2010) discuss some of these losses.

- **Loss of preferred roles**. If you are walking closely with Christ you know who you are and whose you are. You know you are a citizen in heaven, a friend of Christ, an ambassador, a coworker of God, His holy temple, and one with the Father. There is also an identity formation in our own culture such that there are roles we have learned to fill. These must be given up in the new culture and new ones taken on. Missionaries may lose their balance as they have to give up respected aspects of the self and take on new ones that have less perceived value, but are expected in the new culture. When this happens, normal grief may occur, but the missionary may not be aware of the cause since it is so abstract. The ability of the missionary to know his or her identity in Christ will help them greatly during these times, but we must not minimize the pain most people would feel at the loss of familiar cultural roles.

- **Loss of familiar ways of gaining affirmation.** Missionaries have learned to gain affirmation in their own culture in ways that may not work in the new one. The gestures and feedback which tell them they are valued, appreciated, approved of, and accepted are no longer experienced, yet they may not recognize the problem because it is an unconscious process. Instead, they may experience an onslaught of criticism and disdain because they are not measuring up to expectations of the new culture.

- **Losses TCKs experience.** The care team can help the parents recognize the losses their children are experiencing and help them work through it. An excellent resource to understand these losses is *Third Culture Kids* (Pollock and Van Reken, 2009).

God will use these losses to bring deeper reliance on Him. In fact, because of these experiences missionaries seem to have more of a sense of their identity and worth in Him than we do because we rely more naturally on our own culture for these things rather than on Christ. It is truly a joy to know them and to witness the inner peace and security that God works in them after some time through this crucible. However, those newly sent may experience some pain as these cultural familiarities are stripped away and we must lift them up in prayer and be the people there to help bear that burden. The word picture we find for encouragement in the scriptures is "one person joining another on a long journey and speaking words to encourage the traveler to keep going despite obstacles and fatigue." (Wuest, 1975, p. 81) What a beautiful picture of how the church caregiver can minister during these times of normal adjustment.

One Missionary Helps Another

My family and I had been through some good training at Mission Training International (MTI) before we went to the field and one of the things we learned about was the temporary effect of culture shock so that we could identify it in our lives and realize it would pass. When we got there, another new missionary family called me in for help one night when it seemed his family was falling apart. Unfortunately, they had not received any preparatory training so when I prayed with them and assured them that what they were going through was normal, they relaxed and the crisis passed.

Care teams walk a fine line, not wanting to label some of the missionaries' immediate responses to normal stressors on the field as dysfunctional or unspiritual, while at the same time, not wanting to minimize what they're going through when more support is needed

(See MindTheGaps.org for examples of normal stressors in the lives of missionaries). This is what we will explore next.

WHEN DIFFICULTIES OVERWHELM

Cynthia Eriksson conducted research on World Vision aid workers:

> For each of the mental health risk adjustment measures (depression, post traumatic stress disorder and burnout), 30-50 percent of staff scored in the moderate to high risk range. This is a significant amount of people who are working and 'surviving' while experiencing considerable emotional distress. These staff may not be incapacitated by these symptoms presently, but we cannot deny the effect that depression, burnout and Post Traumatic Stress Disorder (PTSD) can have on relationships, work and personal health. (Eriksson, et al., 2003, P. 95)

Likewise, REMAP I and II (Reducing Missionary Attrition Project) found that personal issues such as emotional difficulties and immoral lifestyle, are the highest causes of missionaries returning prematurely from the field, except for unpreventable causes such as retirement, visa problems and illness. (Hay 2007, 12). Research also shows that support in the area of maintaining healthy personal, emotional, and spiritual health is one of the highest factors in preventing missionary attrition. (Hay 2007, 15).

As we look at these statistics we must ask how the church can be an important extra set of eyes to see, ears to hear, and hands to help the missionary who is experiencing intense emotional pain. First, let's look at some situations where it is likely for a missionary to need outside support and/or intervention.

When Missionaries Experience Trauma

When any traumatic experience occurs, there may be specialized responders from the agency, so how is the church care team needed?

There is no diminishing the specialized help these responders can give, but most of us have experienced in a crisis the welcome sight of those we have known all our lives. The church's lifelong relationships with the missionary can be a great comfort by being a listening ear. That can be either in person or by phone on a regular basis, daily to weekly, depending on the severity of the crisis. A substantial amount of our care team's budget is reserved for "boots on the ground" so that one or two from our care team can fly to where the missionaries are to be with them in such a situation. The crisis may include rape or any type of sexual assault, murder, suicide, an attack that threatened someone's life, or trauma impacting a child. You should encourage missionaries to consult with a professional to monitor their emotional state while recovering.

Hostage Crisis

A mission agency called me (William) for a professional consultation with a family whose missionary daughter had been kidnapped by a terrorist group in the Middle East. Not only did they want me to help the family through the trauma, but to help the family remain strong when the terrorists called them, threatening harm to their daughter if money was not sent immediately. Families can become extremely distraught when kidnappers try to make direct contact and increase the threat in the hope of getting more money. One of my roles was to keep the family from trying to negotiate their daughter's release on their own. Thank God she was released, but the end result could have been disastrous if the family did not let the negotiating professionals hired by the mission agency work through the process with the kidnappers.

Thinking about this story later, I realized a need could have been met by a church missionary care team, who would know the missionary and the family and be praying for them. The care team could have been available more often than I was and could be supportive but firm in helping the family trust the hostage negotiators and the mission agency, rather than give in to panic. This scenario will likely become more frequent as missionaries venture into more dangerous situations.

When Missionaries Lose a Loved One

What happens when missionaries lose a loved one, either someone in the primary family of the missionary on the field or extended family at home? Our care team faced this problem on the day a missionary family left for the field and the mother of one of the family members passed away that same day. Decisions had to be made as to whether the family would return immediately, whether part of the family would return, or whether they would wait until they got settled. There were logistical issues of arriving household items, the tremendous cost of a sudden return, and many other issues that can be imagined at such a time.

Although missionaries will want to consult family, friends and their agency, they will almost certainly want to turn to the care team from their sending church for prayer, comfort and advice as to what to do. The care team may be more of an objective sounding board to help the family make such a decision, as was the case here.

Another issue for the care team may be helping the family distinguish between normal grief and progression into depression when they experience loss of a family member or friend. In these situations we as Christians do not feel sorrow as others who have no hope, but we still experience feelings of grief. Those close to the missionary can watch for signs when normal grief turns into incapacitating pain.

GUIDELINES FOR NORMAL VS. ABNORMAL GRIEF

- Normal emotions of emptiness and loss are most intense immediately after the loss, then decrease as time passes, coming in waves or pangs, usually as a result of reminders and thoughts of the deceased loved one. Abnormal depression shows up in depressed mood, self-critical or pessimistic thoughts with inability to experience happiness or pleasure.
- Positive emotions and humor associated with happy memories of the loved one are part of the pain of normal grief which are uncharacteristic of the pervasive unhappiness and misery found in depression.

- Self esteem is preserved in normal grief as opposed to the self-denigration and feelings of worthlessness found in depression. Some self-derogatory thoughts can be present in normal grief, but they are usually tied to guilt over not spending enough time with the deceased or not expressing love prior to death.
- Thoughts about death occur, but the thoughts are usually focused on the deceased and joining that person in heaven. The depressed person's thoughts of death center on ending the pain of depression, worthlessness, and not deserving to live through suicide. (Diagnostic & Statistical Manual of Mental Disorders, 5th Edition, p.126).

If normal symptoms of bereavement become entrenched over a long period of time and are exacerbated, then professional consultation should be obtained by the care team in conjunction with the agency as to not duplicate efforts.

WHEN MISSIONARIES HIDE THEIR PAIN

When there is no obvious precipitating event, how do we as church caregivers notice that a missionary's emotional state is overwhelming or incapacitating? Some may ask if that gap of care is one we need to fill. Will the agency care professionals be the first to notice these symptoms and find the missionary help? Not necessarily. The same independent spirit that God used to give our missionaries the ability to leave all and go to the field can also work against them to not seek outside help when needed.

THE MISSIONARY CULTURE OF INDEPENDENCE

I Don't Want to Be a Complainer

We knew we were going to encounter more difficulties in life than usual when we signed up to minister in another culture. So, naturally, when we feel overwhelmed, even for an extended period

> of time, we don't want to be seen as complainers, and don't want those who sent us to think we're not up to the job. So, we get through it as best we can, with God's help.

A pastor we know observed that when missionaries are in trouble, they "hunker down and get weird." Though that is not a flattering description, it may sometimes be what happens. There is a culture of independence which keeps some missionaries from reaching out to find the support or help they need. Our Christian culture needs to become more comfortable with the normalcy of brokenness so that all Christians, including missionaries, can come to one another for encouragement and support in whatever place they find themselves.

This can, indeed, be a gap of care. We need to position ourselves in our missionaries' lives to be able to notice when emotional pain overwhelms them. To do this we must successfully work with the culture of independence. How do we do this? We have found that if we have been demonstrating that we care all along, sometimes it's just a case of being there at the right time and place where the missionary opens up to us. Bringing our missionaries together on a yearly retreat where common experiences promote vulnerable sharing is sometimes the right time and place. Spending personal time with them, just hanging out when they are at home is a great way to be there at the right time and place. Having more structured dinners to help them debrief where the care team asks specific questions on how they're doing in various areas of their lives gives another opportunity to be at the right time and place. By visiting them on the field we can see what they go through and how they respond. This is the most effective way to be at the right time and place for them to open up to us.

EXAMINE OURSELVES AS CAREGIVERS

What can be done if, despite our best efforts, the missionary seems to shun our desire to listen or get help? It may be useful to do some self-examination at this point. Scott Schaum from Barnabas International, gives a good perspective on being present with them in times of emotional pain.

> "...we must be mindful of two temptations. First, we like to be needed. However, *what people really need is Christ (emphasis ours)*. Our goal needs to be bringing Christ to the person, and the person to Christ. Secondly, we like to fix stuff. Please, do not try to fix people or their problems. Whatever may need to be "fixed," it will be helped by love and accompaniment. God will deliver them when the time is right. My primary role is to be a companion in this process. There is no greater gift we can give someone suffering than our simple, abiding, enduring presence." (Schaefer and Schaefer, 2013).

We must also look at the possibility that the missionary may not need conversation as much as to be cared for in some practical way (See chapter 12 on Practical Needs).

HELP YOUR RESISTANT MISSIONARY

There may be some occasions where you feel a more direct approach is needed. Here is a protocol if you feel a missionary is in need of outside help and is still resisting it, despite your best efforts.

- Identify the problem, describing your concern for how this affects them.
- Give them some options for help, along with costs and logistics.
- Ask them to pray about it and determine what part they are willing to do.
- Tell them you will follow up to see what they decided.

OUR RESILIENT MISSIONARIES

Fortunately, the church is aligning itself more with the scriptural truth that we are all broken, including His chosen workers, and more missionaries are transparent and able to seek help when they need it.

> **A Family Crisis — Jumped In**
> We were on furlough and about to go back to our host country when a severe crisis occurred with one of our children. Conventional wisdom for such a crisis was that it would take months of counseling to resolve the issue. A counselor on our church's missionary care team was able to see us right away and was able to meet with us for some short term, intensive counseling that enabled us to resolve the issue well enough to return as a family to the field. Later, I shared with the counselor how we were at such a loss to know what to do when we had only a short time and how grateful we were that she was willing to jump in and see what the Lord could do.

Though the bad news is that missionaries suffer significantly more hardship and trauma than the rest of us, the good news is that missionaries typically are resilient people. In fact, research shows that as a group, they can endure a lot more stress and emotional pain and still remain resilient than the average person (Schaeffer, et al. 2007). This is one of the reasons missionary care is so enjoyable to many of us. They inspire us as we see them remain dedicated, sacrificial, and resilient in the face of pain and difficulties, as they rely on God.

According to Karen Carr of the Mobile Member Care Team in West Africa (MMCT) "Resilience is having strength to fulfill the call God has given us, even when it will be painful and difficult. Resilience is staying fixed on a higher purpose, motivated by love of God, our neighbor, and the world, *and supported by friends* (emphasis ours)" (Schaefer and Schaefer 2012, 93).

Let *us* be those friends in their times of emotional need.

GET ON BOARD

Here are some guidelines and questions as we end this section on how to respond to both the normal and the overwhelming pain in a missionary's life.

1. In the case of normal adjustments in a missionary's life, they just need for us to acknowledge the pain and be a good listener to help share the burden. What are some situations you've encountered in a missionary's life that could be understood as normal adjustments? How did you and/or others in your church react to it?

2. Be aware of the missionary culture of independence which may cause some missionaries not to report or to minimize overwhelming pain when it happens. How well do your missionaries admit to problems and ask for help? How can your care team create an environment to make it easy for them to do so?

3. Build trusting relationships with your missionaries as a foundation to promote openness when the time comes for more support. What ways can you position yourselves for spontaneous ministry to take place?

4. In times of crisis or trauma, how comfortable are you to be present with your missionary in the midst of intense emotional pain? What means will you use — email, Skype, phone, or field visit?

5. Rehearse a scenario with your team using the protocol as outlined in The Resistant Missionary.

Chapter 12

Practical Needs

Sue Hood and Bill & Betty Jane Born

A Life Saved

With a phone call, a doctor from a church was able to intervene in what turned out to be a potentially deadly situation in which medical help could not be obtained. The doctor was able to advise the couple regarding the seriousness of the situation and guide them in the lifesaving steps to prevent possible death. It was the strong tie with their sending church that enabled them to reach out in an emergency when they weren't sure what to do.

Our Trinity Missionary Care Team Purpose Statement as presented in Chapter 2 promotes the wellbeing, growth, effectiveness and sustainability of Trinity's missionaries through facilitating the meeting of physical, spiritual and emotional needs. This chapter specifically addresses many of those physical needs in practical ways.

God, our Jehovah Jireh, the God who provides, takes pleasure in meeting the various needs of his global workers. Sometimes a gap of care is created by an emergency and, as with most of us, we turn to those close to us for help. It is the church that is uniquely equipped, with all categories of willing and generous people of varied talents, professions and resources to help our missionaries in practical ways. What an encouragement it is to have their practical needs met through the very people who sent them and have a heart for their well-being. Here are some ways the church can organize the resources God has given them to benefit their missionary family.

ORGANIZING A RESOURCE LIST

To engage the congregation as one of our core values, we compiled a list of ways the congregation could be involved. Then we created opportunities for people to sign up where they would like to serve when needs arose, with the understanding that they could decline, should their circumstances dictate. Finally, from this information we made a master list of names to help with needs for doctors, dentists, nurses, teachers, babysitters, learning specialists, computer techs, and those willing to provide vehicles or housing (see our Resource List Template at MindTheGaps.org). Congregations usually have people who would not be able to go overseas, yet are excited to bless the missionaries with their talents and resources. A yearly update of this list is helpful to assess the willingness of each individual as life brings changes.

When our missionaries want to access the list, we ask them to contact the care team first, then we contact the potential volunteer to find out if that resource is still available. We keep track of which volunteers have been used lately so that we can spread the needs around.

Furlough and Re-Entry Help

> **Not Homeless (Bill and Betty Jane)**
> We have had varied furlough housing experiences during our 42 years as missionaries. On one furlough, a women's group generously stocked a pantry at our church's mission house with food and other supplies for our family. I was absolutely overwhelmed as I saw items we all loved that they could not have known about, but that the Lord was pleased to provide through them.

When a missionary family returns to the U.S. on furlough, for a time before reassignment, or when leaving mission service, they need special care and help. The missionary care team will meet with them to provide personal care and support, help them access the Resource List for housing, car and other needs, and will continue that contact while they are in the U.S. In our regular missionary prayer group (see

Chapter 6) we begin praying for our missionaries' furlough needs several months before they come. Certainly housing and transportation are their two biggest needs, but there are others as well.

Housing Needs

This is a significant need each time a missionary returns home. Living with family is nice for a week or two, but not usually best for the duration of a furlough. A typical home is not big enough for two families to share over an extended time. A wonderful provision is a furnished house or apartment. A positive childhood memory church families can give their children is cleaning, painting and fixing up a house for a missionary family.

Transportation Needs

Dependable transportation, and a car seat if necessary, is always essential. Our church maintains two vehicles for use by our missionaries on a first come, first serve basis. Besides that, missionaries can access our Resource List for a car. If it's a long furlough and funds are available, the missionary could buy a used car, possibly from a church member, and then sell it just before leaving for the field again. On occasion, we have noticed the temptation for churches or individuals to provide a car no one would want.

Kids' Needs

Our mission house has a collection of toys and bikes, and there is also an association swimming pool available with the house. Theme park tickets make a nice gift (our church is near Disneyland). With a large family, we helped our children to be comfortable on furloughs by providing each child with his own sleeping bag, pillow and stuffed animal. With that, sleeping was never an issue no matter where they needed to sleep.

Clothing Needs

Jackets and winter clothing are a necessary item that the church can provide. When stocking the mission house kitchen for an arriving family, it is nice to have the beds ready, and gifts of clothing or other items can be put on each appropriate bed.

All Decked Out

One furlough I (Betty Jane) received a very generous gift of new, stylish clothes from a church member. Though very grateful, I remember feeling uncomfortable with the unfamiliar styles, until I overheard a comment from someone that was at the conference where I spoke. She said I was the most stylish missionary there.

Financial Support

Besides praying and funding the ministries of church missionaries, there are additional ways for a church and its missionary care team to encourage their missionaries in this important aspect of their ministry.

We found this to be an all too common gap for the care team to step in and fill, so much so that we asked two people to join our team who had experience in helping missionaries who were struggling in this area. Low financial support has the potential to bring them off the field, so when we hear musings of discouragement regarding finances from any of our missionaries we offer assistance right away. We find out where their difficulties are, brainstorm ideas to increase contacts, and collaborate with them as they write support letters.

Also, there are ways a person on the care team can link missionaries and pastors together. When your missionary is fundraising for the first time in his career, your pastoral staff can introduce him to other pastors in the area. The more support a missionary raises in the home area, the more exposure your church will have with its missionary as it limits the need for widespread travel each time the missionary returns from overseas.

Soon after a new pastor and/or new mission committee member is appointed, they should personally take initiative to know their missionaries and understand each ministry. A purposeful field visit or extended Skype call to each missionary during the early years of a pastor's tenure would be most encouraging not only to the missionary, but to the pastor and through him to the entire congregation.

Dropped!

One missionary experienced a great relationship with their supporting church for over thirty-five years. There were awards and

> personal gifts given and warm relationships throughout that time until a new pastor notified them that they would be dropped from the church's support within twelve months, even though they had only five years left of service. It was a difficult five years as they struggled to make up the difference and finally received full support — just two months before retirement.

Gifts

Christmas gifts or money cards are appreciated, and lets the missionary know that they are valued. A larger Christmas project would be a "Christmas Missionary of the Year" when the missionary family is honored with a special service to present gifts purchased by the church body.

Presenting a camp scholarship to the family if their visit coincides with a church camp would be a great gift, possibly making the difference whether children are able to attend or not.

Cost of Living Increases

As a missionary, my husband and I (Sue) had twelve supporting churches, but only one church gave us a yearly cost of living increase. Over the years, those increases were very significant. Including these increases yearly could help reduce the amount of time a missionary family must be in the U.S. raising support.

Medical Needs

On several occasions, when one of our missionary families living in a remote location needed medical advice, one of the doctors in our church communicated with them by internet until they were able to locate appropriate help. Dental or orthodontic help could be offered at reduced cost during furlough years. The myriad of resources a church is able to offer, however, depends on the size and resources of the congregation. If your church members desire to provide such services, they should be included on the Resource List so that your missionaries know they are available. Should the required expertise not lie within your congregation, church members can contact doctors and dentists in their community and ask if they could help. Pray and network on their behalf.

Educational Needs

When good schooling options are not available to an overseas missionary family, home schooling becomes a possibility. However, for many missionaries that option can be overwhelming. "For any type of homeschooling or correspondence and online schools, parents must have access to educational tools, technology, and other resources in order to do a good job." (Pollock and Van Reken 2009, 203). In our church, some educators and home school moms have offered to assist missionary families in the choice of curriculum, encouragement throughout the school year, and assistance with special education needs that might surface.

Another need a church can provide for a college TCK is tuition assistance. Our children attended a Christian college that would match a church gift up to $1000 each year of college for missionary enrollees. That was a significant blessing since our students paid their own school costs.

God has abundant resources in His kingdom to meet the practical needs of His global workers. Become intentional and willing with heart-filled love for your missionaries. Just like the boy with five loaves and two fishes who had a willing heart, God will multiply the resources through you that He has for His workers.

GET ON BOARD

1. After your church begins to demonstrate interest in helping their mission families, develop a resource list where the congregation can offer to help with skills that may be needed. Make annual adjustments to the list (see MindTheGaps.org).

2. Six months before your next missionary returns home, ask what needs they will have. Pray with them for God's provision and determine what needs and surprises your church can provide.

3. Does your missionary have financial needs, or need for increased monthly support? How may you as a care team encourage your church to help? Use your creativity to assist and consider other area churches that might also help.

Chapter 13

Professional Effectiveness Needs

Bill Born, William Britt and David Wilson

An effective missionary is a happy missionary. Just like any other professional, a missionary has the need to succeed and bear fruit. As the church seeks to care for its missionaries, professional effectiveness should be a priority. This chapter will provide a framework for your care team to consider as you invest your time, talents and energy to help your global workers thrive.

INCREASING EFFECTIVENESS THROUGH TRAINING

At Trinity Church, we require all of our missionaries to go through pre-field missionary candidate training either through their sending agency or through a specialized cross-cultural training organization. There are a number of highly qualified and experienced training facilities which specialize in pre-field missionary training (see MindTheGaps.org for a current list of training institutions). Some agencies offer an "orientation" to the field, but we have found that a more intensive and interactive training is needed for first-term missionaries, and even more so for missionaries who have been on the field, but left because of problems. Often, orientation is synonymous with 'how to raise financial support' or 'learn about the demographics of your destination'. Though these things are critical aspects of missionary training, missionaries need much more time and information to help them stay on the field and be successful.

Whether you send your missionary family to a training organization, or if their agency provides training, ask to see the topics that are covered, the duration of their training and check reviews of those who have experience in this field. Like everything else in life, there is helpful training and there is not-so-helpful training. Here are the key topics to look for in good quality pre-field missionary training:

- Team Building and Leadership
- Cross Cultural Adaptation
- Language Acquisition
- Financial Support
- Sharpening Interpersonal Skills
- Spiritual Formation: Self, Family, Third Culture Kids (TCK) needs
- Ministry Methods: Church Planting, Teaching English as a Second Language (ESL), Poverty Alleviation, and Medical/ Dental
- Contingency Planning with Crisis Intervention

All of these topics fit within one of the following three categories: Knowledge *(Head)*, Character *(Heart)* and Skills *(Hands)*. A sending church will do well to seriously evaluate missionary candidates on the basis of their head, heart and hands. Missionary attrition rates during the first term of service vary depending on the agency, denomination and the particular field of ministry, but rates improve when pre-field training is provided. (Britt, 1980)

The causes of missionary attrition can be categorized as: Dropouts, Burnouts, Forceouts, Washouts, and Never-should-have-Goneouts (IFMA April, 1998). The Dropouts are those who began training but didn't make it to the field. They realized that the life of a missionary was going to be too much for them to handle. The Burnouts actually make it to the field, but soon discover that the stress and demands of living on the field are beyond their ability to cope. The Forceouts are those who leave the field due to uncontrollable factors such as health, finances, visa issues or regional instability. The Washouts are generally missionaries who fail to get along with their team or their sending agency. We know of missionaries who have bounced from agency to agency, from team to team and from country to country because they just do not cope well with others. We hear phrases like: "We wanted more freedom to pursue our personal ministry objective" or "Our goals were not in alignment with the rest of the team" or "We have irreconcilable differences with a certain team member." These may be legitimate claims, but they may also indicate a problem if a pattern begins to form.

Training helps to remove some rigid and inflexible tendencies that are built into many western missionaries. Not only does it help prepare missionaries for a more flexible lifestyle and work ethic, but it also serves as a screening mechanism for those who should not go out onto the field. This may come as a surprise, but just because someone says that they feel called by the Lord does not mean that they are called to go to the mission field. This calling may be to youth ministry in a local church, or to non-profit work in the inner city, or to work in the secular world while serving as a volunteer on the missionary care team.

In Acts 13, we see a very healthy way of understanding someone's call. Paul and Barnabas were 'called' by the Lord to a mission. This call was heard by the church leaders when the Holy Spirit spoke to others in the church as well. The church fasted and prayed about this which implies it was not an immediate sending, but they took time to discern the Lord's call. Once all the preparations were in place, they laid hands on them, prayed and sent them off.

If, in the process of candidate preparation and training, your church leaders conclude that your candidate does not have what it takes to be a missionary, then the church should not send him/her. Too often, churches and agencies make irrational decisions just so they can mobilize more people on the field, not realizing that some people may do more harm than good if they are not the right fit. This is hard to hear, but consider these examples: Would you want someone who has a problem with alcohol to be your pilot? Do you want someone with anger problems to be your surgeon? Why would we send someone who is inflexible and rigid to be a representative of God's kingdom in the Middle East? We need to have high standards and expectations of our missionaries. Beware of phrases like "I just don't fit anywhere else, so I think God is calling me to be a missionary" or "I think being a missionary will be easy compared to working in the corporate world", or my favorite is "Everywhere I have lived and every job I have held has left me unhappy, so I think God is leading me to move overseas and be a missionary." All of the above quotes were said in the context of interviews for missionary candidates and they were all very sincere.

God's call on the life of a missionary is critical to his long term success on the field (see ReMAP). When things are tough, his call experience will be the one thing that keeps him on the field. His sense of call is the difference between thriving and surviving in difficult circumstances.

How does this relate to church based missionary care? One of the most caring things we can do for people is help guide them to the right place in God's kingdom. That is why the care team needs to be involved with missionary candidates from the very beginning. They should know what life is like on the field. Their relationships with missionaries help to guide decisions based on experience with people who are capable of surviving the rigors of the missionary life.

If your church has the right people resources for a church based missionary candidate team, Greg Carter has developed curriculum for pre-field missionary training called *Skills, Knowledge, Character: A Church-Based Approach to Missionary Candidate Preparation* (Carter 2010). This resource will guide your missionary candidates through a process which will help your church leaders discover the strengths and weaknesses of the new missionary — we all have both. Through the coaching/mentoring relationship, the missionary builds confidence in strengths and a realistic understanding of his weaknesses. This enables him to build a strong bond with his mentor which becomes a strength while on the field. Because strength and weaknesses are revealed, the care team can be aware of them as the missionary is deployed.

INCREASING EFFECTIVENESS THROUGH ACCOUNTABILITY

One of the most challenging aspects of missionary care, especially regarding effectiveness, is the tension between caring and holding others accountable. We have tried to focus on the caring, but experience has taught us that sometimes part of caring is accountability. Here are some examples:

A Distraught Missionary

What do you do if you make a field visit and find your missionary in tears, sensing she might be failing, hasn't learned the language, does not have a ministry, and then in the next few days of the visit you discover this is true? In the midst of being with your distraught missionary, you have to decide how serious the situation is, and if the missionary is truly failing, what steps to take. Grace and truth are the banks of the river of love. If the grace bank fails, then you have truth without grace which can be hard, demanding and cold. If the truth bank fails, then you have empathy, tenderness, caring, but no truth or accountability, which leads to aimless wandering and floundering in defeat.

Do you request they leave the field? Do you contact their agency? Do you leave them in despair? Our approach has been to look for the gaps, attempt to address them, and then leave the dignity of the missionary intact as much as possible. For example, we tried to determine where the communication with the agency had failed, for it appeared the missionary had been neglected both in supervision and training by the agency. In this case, we encouraged our missionary to contact the agency and let them know the desperate situation she was in, rather than tell her that we would report her to the agency or make her come home ourselves, which would further undermine her fragile self-esteem. We encouraged her to let her agency know of the difficulty she was having learning the language, and the gaps in training which prevented her from having a successful ministry. We also let her know we would follow up with the agency to encourage them to provide appropriate assistance.

In this case, her financial support was low, and we helped her plan when she could leave the field without damaging her ministry, also recognizing that the process of developing further support would be a test of her effectiveness as she presented her ministry successes and failures to current and future financial supporters. We trusted that God would then confirm her call, or show her that perhaps He had other plans for her. She was resistant to hearing some of these accurate but painful assessments, and it required a balance of truth and grace to keep the love flowing within the banks.

The Missionary Compound

Some of us have heard the tragic tales of missionaries who have had a conflict and then refuse to speak to one another for 20 years, almost forgetting the content of the original conflict. An involved missionary care team would have a relationship with at least one of the missionaries to the degree that they could intervene in such a situation. The team would go to the field to work with them to prevent the missionary from a premature return from the field. In earlier days, travel cost and pride would have kept them on the field.

The Desperate Missionary Housewife

There may be issues of effectiveness that affect the missionary wife who becomes depressed because of caring for the children and failing to learn the language. Her husband is out doing ministry, developing relationships, improving language skills, feeling fulfilled, and oblivious to his wife's suffering at home. She has no adult relationships apart from him, because she has not learned the language sufficiently to make friends.

She cannot shop because the language barrier keeps her from using local transportation and bargaining in the market, so her husband has to perform this task. She is left isolated with their children, sinking deeper into a depression that she dare not share with her husband because it may mean the failure of their mission. The mission agency sees the reports from the husband and assumes everything is fine, since he is unaware of her growing despondency. It is only after she completely shuts down and cannot function that he realizes she has been protecting him from the truth, and the whole family must come home. She then has to be hospitalized because of the severity of the depression, and their missionary career comes to an end. The number of times this has occurred in our experience must mean it is more widespread than we realize.

What if there is a missionary care team from her church who cares about her effectiveness, communicates with her regularly, and notices her discouragement before it turns into depression? What if someone encourages her to learn the language, to go out and take risks with nationals, to work at meeting other women and couples, who welcomes her honest sharing at any time, and comes to visit to see how the family is doing? A healthy intervention would be to confront the husband who is so focused on ministry that he forgets his first priority is caring for and discipling his family. The care team holds him accountable during the future months and years. The mission agency may never be aware of the crisis that was averted by a home church who keeps love flowing along high banks of grace and truth.

Our view of effectiveness is often different from that of the mission agency. The agency tends to care more about the effectiveness on the field and the end results. The church-based care team model strives to care more about how the missionary is doing personally, emotionally and relationally, not just the field results. Each of these vignettes was either not spotted by the agency or did not rise to the level of concern until it was too late. An active care team would discover such gaps and hopefully prevent such calamities.

INCREASING EFFECTIVENESS THROUGH COMMUNICATION

What is the communication role of the missionary care team? So much has been said and written about this word — communication. We have seminars, videos, degree programs, books as well as lots and lots of talk about it. We communicate every day all day long. Communication is the lubricant of life. When there is a sufficient amount of communication, things go smoothly. When there is a lack of it, there is friction. A missionary care team can be a remarkable agent of help in the effectiveness and longevity of missionaries by the frequency and variety of supportive communication. Bear in mind that communication must be a two-way street. Without listeners, conversation becomes a silent monologue – like a speaker in a sound proof room with no one present. When words fall on deaf ears, communication goes nowhere.

A missionary care team must know their missionary, the one with whom they are speaking. The ideal situation is when the missionary care team and the missionary become like a healthy, loving and thriving family. Quality communication is the mark of a good family. "A healthy family communicates and listens. Without genuine listening and sharing of ourselves we can't know each other. The family needs to have permission to name, own and express feelings without being punished" (Curran 1983, 9).

How valuable is hearing from folks at home to a missionary? Having served as a missionary myself (Bill), be assured that your communication has an effective power. Messages that arrive when someone is feeling forgotten can actually bolster a lonely missionary for continued months. Perhaps the missionary has even been dealing with an attack of the enemy, who is always working to discourage the child of God. Your words can be the antidote in a specific time of attack. My personal experiencc has shown me over and over how important it is to hear from those who know and love me. I also observed the excitement of "…good news from a far country" that others display when they receive personal mail. Mine was the privilege of delivering the mail bag to missionaries in remote areas.

Precious Cargo Called 'Mail'

It had been over two weeks since the airplane visited their jungle post. There was an anticipated excitement as, by short wave radio, they reported the weather condition with an emphasis of a beautiful day with no expectation of rain. For these precious ones presenting the good news of Jesus Christ and His word it was "flight day." Today they would receive invaluable supplies to sustain their work in a remote village. The delivery would always include food, fuel and a large variety of items to sustain them for several weeks. Sometimes it was a sewing machine from Czechoslovakia, and other times it was even a kitchen sink.

The missionaries were always excited as the plane arrived. There were greetings and catching up on just how each person was. Next was unloading the cargo and carrying it to their homes. If you could hide somewhere without being seen you would observe something of significance. If the mailbag was among the cargo but not visible, the missionaries would be close to the door always looking for their precious mailbag. If, instead it was the first thing given to them, there was a visible sigh of relief and smiles of great joy. From your invisible place you too would smile as you saw their joy in receiving their long-awaited mail. Important to the missionaries? — That is an understatement! By the way, as a pilot it quickly became your worst day ever if you forgot the mail.

PRUDENT COMMUNICATION

Today, using wisdom as we communicate with our global missionaries requires awareness of world conditions particularly in the countries which have restricted access and are closed to the gospel. Perhaps nowhere is this more important than in email and social media, because it can be monitored, retrieved, and used to incriminate senders or receivers. Avoid writing about political and religious issues. Extra care and wisdom is required in communication with workers in closed countries. Your worker will help you understand the particular situation, but please do not allow this to be a hindrance from communicating. Those working in this context need encouragement as much, if not more, than others. Following is a sample of communication guidelines from one of our workers serving in a restricted access nation:

Communication Guidelines for Missionaries in a Muslim Context

The word "missionary" has different connotations for different people. In the Muslim world, missionaries are often seen as the ones that come in and change their culture, heritage, and way of life in a negative way. This is not what we want to communicate about our identity because it is not who we are. We are followers of Jesus who seek to love those whom He loves and to live in a way which glorifies God. Please help us maintain our identity to others by following these guidelines.

When communicating with us, please do not:

- Use these words: Missions, Missionary, Converts, Baptism, War
- Talk about politics or criticize the government leaders in our country
- Use the name of our agency
- Forward newsletters or prayer letters of other cross-cultural workers
- Speak ill of Muhammad or the Qur'an

Feel free to use general spiritual words such as God, Pray, Jesus, Bible, and Qur'an. Muslims believe and do these things as well. We would love for the church to pray for us, and we want folks to know what is going on in our world.

However, for our safety, please do not:

- Post our names, picture, or country of residence on the internet
- Place a copy of printed materials that have our names and picture on the internet
- Put our names and description of our work on the internet or in print

- Display our names in connection with our agency
- Display our newsletters at the church or on any website

Don't let these guidelines keep you from communicating! Thank you for your respect in following them. They are necessary for our safety and the safety of those with whom we work. If you have any questions about any of these please let us know.

At Trinity Church, we now have a one page "Communication Guidelines" form for all of our missionaries, regardless of where they are in the world. For some it is as simple as, "we prefer communicating via text messages" and for others we have all of the various forms of communication along with user names and addresses. Missionaries are mostly honored when a church asks them to list communication expectations and guidelines, because it tells them that someone cares enough to communicate.

METHODS OF COMMUNICATING

If you lived from the year 1900 until 2000 you would have lived in a period of history where there had been more technological development than in all previous centuries combined. Methods of communication are among the many advancements which have changed the way we interact with our missionaries, and they continue to change and improve. We fully expect that communication technology will continue to advance, even in the short time between the writing of this chapter and the publishing of this book. Although methods change, the purpose of communication does not change. Here is a brief anthology of communication methods from this last generation of missionaries serving on the field right now.

Letters — In spite of modern technology, this method remains viable and continues to be well utilized. With the advent of air travel and private letter carriers like UPS, FedEx, and DHL, possibilities exist for international delivery of items in a matter of days. Regardless of changes in methods of delivery, those little envelopes with the name of the recipient, and a stamp with a return address remain a consistent joy that lights up the far corners of the missionary world.

Care Packages — Parcels from home are a great way to bless your missionary. Keep the packages small to avoid high customs fees. Any size package will bring joy. Choose personal items that will not spoil or tempt anyone to pilfer. Enjoy the creativity of assembling a two to four pound box with wonderful reminders from home. Ask your missionary, or the agency, about delivery times, and mail special occasion packages in advance to assure timely delivery.

Audio/Video — If your missionary is able to receive CDs or DVDs, send them a sermon, music or movie disk. It is a thoughtful way to encourage parents and children. Always verify if they have the right equipment to play U.S. made digital media, since many countries of the world use a different format (for example, Europe uses PAL for their DVD format while the U.S. has NTSC). Though it is nice to receive items in the mail, the internet is also a great way to give the gift of Audio/Video. A simple email with a link to an online sermon may be a way for your missionary to stay connected to the body. Music is now in 'the cloud' so there is not much need for CDs any more. Send your missionary a pre-loaded MP3 player along with a gift card so that they can purchase music from any place on earth where they can find an internet connection. Digital readers and eBooks make excellent gifts so that missionaries can download the most recent books. A gift card for their eReader would not only be thoughtful, but a very practical gift to help them stay current, intellectually sharp, culturally relevant and missionally effective on their field.

Short Wave or Ham Radio — There are many individuals who enjoy Ham Radio as a hobby and willingly assist missionaries in long-distance communication. Over the years this has been and continues to be a wonderful source of voice communication in remote areas of the world. By means of a 'phone patch' this tool allows remote missionaries to communicate with family, loved ones and churches a continent away. I (David) remember when I was in the military serving in the Mediterranean region, and got a phone patch to speak with my wife back home. Some hobbyist in another part of the world provided the switch to facilitate our conversation. I would say something like "Hello beautiful…over" and she would respond with "Hello, how are you doing?… over." The word 'over' was the switchman's cue to open the path for the other person to speak. Obviously, communication was a little awkward, and there was no privacy since you knew someone was listening, but it was clear communication. For people in extremely remote environments like rainforests, jungles, desert, and even war zones or refugee camps, where other forms of communication do not exist, this is one of the best ways to keep in touch.

FAX — This is generally used for documents that need to be signed for legal purposes and sent over telephone lines. Missionaries on the field are frequently in need of someone back home to serve as proxy for matters of estate, wills, and trusts, and other legal documents. This is a much needed gap which a missionary care team could fill, so perhaps a better option today is the office scanner to produce a PDF which can be emailed over the internet. This is a bit more secure and reliable, but not always accessible. As a missionary care team the method must be thought through and used wisely.

Telephone/Mobile Phone — Communication via telephone today is, for the most part, quick, clear and affordable. It is a wonderful way to encourage your missionary. This modern tool is available all over the world and works extremely well.

It's a Boy!

When our first child was born in Brazil it was my (Bill) joy and responsibility to run to the telephone company to call our parents informing them of their new grandson. Four hours later and after multiple attempts I walked out of the booth at the telephone company with a sense of frustration, exhaustion and a degree of numbness in my head and heart. I was never certain that our parents heard me say "It's a boy," let alone catch any of the details. Regardless, whether they heard me or not, it was a very expensive long distance call.

Because of the expensive nature of landlines, the wired phone is used less overseas than the more affordable mobile phone. Some of the most humorous experiences we have had on mission journeys is seeing people in remote places of the earth using a mobile phone. Bedouin tribes in North Africa, peasant fishermen in Southeast Asia, and cattlemen on the Pampas in Argentina all have mobile phones. Today's missionaries are fortunate to have this technology in most every corner of the world and it should be used to its maximum benefit by missionary care teams. Some missionaries in extremely remote areas of the world will have satellite phones, but they are very expensive.

Internet Video Calls – There are free, online video conferencing tools which most church mission groups can use to communicate with their workers on the field. It is instant, visual and personal. Often a church will have a live call during a prayer meeting or worship service. The communication connects the hearts and eyes of congregation with their missionary and can be a huge encouragement. Security is always an issue, so use caution and wisdom as you communicate. For mental health professionals, do proper research to determine HIPAA compliance via any form of electronic and video communication. The rules change and the technology changes, so make sure you have up-to-date knowledge of best practices in this field. (see MindTheGaps.org for an updated list of communication tools and current technology)

Email — Prayer requests can be received and responded to in the same hour with email. Missionaries can have prayer chains activated instantly. Email has changed how families and loved ones maintain contact which allows for both a quantity and a quality of communication. This effective tool has helped missionaries exist in very difficult situations for the long term. However, there is one great big, ominous and menacing down side to email communication. Because the communication is so fast and can be shared, forwarded and duplicated like a virus, it carries the inherent dangers of misinterpretation, breech of privacy and compromise of security. Individuals, field teams and entire organizations have been ruined by the power of the 'send' button (McCulley, 2000).

Social Media – New forms of communication are being introduced to us everyday. From websites to mobile phone apps, we have the ability to connect in remarkable ways. Technology is moving at such a rapid pace, that if we list what is available today, it may not be available tomorrow. Actually, SnapChat is one of many interesting forms of communication where a picture appears for a limited time only, and then it disappears. Facebook has been serving our global workers well since 2004, but we are seeing a decline in the future of its usability. Regardless of the technology of the day, some caution needs to be observed; mainly, the rule of triangulation. This happens when someone identifies missionaries in a way that compromises their work. For example, posting a photo of a missionary on Facebook with their name and place of service may be dangerous if they are serving in Pakistan, Yemen or another restricted access nation. Churches should teach their congregants how to interact with missionaries in a way that does not harm the work on the field or the people involved in the work. Sometimes, the worst thing that happens to the missionary is that their visa is revoked, but the danger of physical harm to those nationals who are closely aligned with the missionary is a real threat.

On-Field Personal Visits — Of all the methods of communication, this is the very best because it includes all the essential elements of communication—personal interaction, listening without judgment, caring, relating, empathizing and the exchange of ideas, to name a few. Nothing affirms another more than taking a personal interest in them and their ministry in person. The most important aspect of our visit is spending quality time talking with them and seeing their work firsthand. Missionaries are very busy, so we negotiate a meeting agenda with them before our arrival, so that we can have intentional, face to face, and uninterrupted time to go deep in conversation that transcends discussions about the climate, culture and conditions on the field. Don't allow the missionaries to keep you busy sightseeing, since that may be a signal that there is something they are trying to ignore in their personal lives. Give them opportunities to be vulnerable and transparent, since they may not have anyone else in their lives who is safe enough with whom to confide. The purpose in visiting a missionary is not to do sightseeing, but to invest all your time for the encouragement of those you are visiting. Make that clear with your missionary ahead of time and communicate your intentions so that they will feel honored and respected.

GET ON BOARD

1. Choose how and when you will communicate with your missionaries. Ask what items they can and cannot receive. Find out how long a package takes to reach them.

2. Decide the frequency your care team wants to visit your missionaries. Space trips on a calendar over several years. Include those ministering in your home country. Take note of details regarding field visits included throughout this book.

3. Gather information from your missionaries on items they may appreciate receiving in packages.

PART FIVE

Changing Tracks

Transitions

Chapter 14

Changes Within Ministry

Linda Parker

Transitions are a normal part of life. If you have a family, you will resonate with the common feeling that you're always in transition. Children are born, become teenagers, grow up and leave home. Mothers or fathers believe they're better suited for a different career and move their families. Stay-at-home moms go to work when kids are in school to help pay increasing expenses.

Missionaries are ordinary people who go through these transitions, too. When children become teenagers, the family may want to be reassigned to a place that provides more appropriate schooling. Health problems may require a different climate and better medical care. When the teenagers enter college, missionary parents sometimes elect to come home to support them through those important years. Some may go to the field, serving in one ministry and find that God is calling them to a different ministry, whether or not their work is completed. Some are not ready to leave their host country and ministry but are forced out because of visa problems or political unrest. For these and other reasons, they may change countries, ministries, agencies or teams, and God is sovereign in leading His workers through all of it.

Transitions can be messy. Saying goodbye to people you have given your sweat, tears and heart to can be difficult. There may be unresolved issues (i.e. interpersonal conflict or questioning one's effectiveness) that can become emotional baggage in the next assignment. New languages and cultures may need to be learned in the next assignment, and the home church needs to endorse the new endeavor as well.

In this chapter, we will look at what missionaries and their children experience during these changes and how we in the church can support them in the transitions they face. We've asked missionaries from around the world to describe their experiences of transition. At the end of each segment there will be questions to help you understand their experience.

Leaving So Soon?

After five years in the culture, just when I began to feel like this really was my home, God began to move my heart in another direction. I felt it would be a failure if I stepped away, just as God was opening up new doors in our zone. After interceding for a people; after fighting through ongoing warfare and discouragement with a team; after seeing God bring small bits of fruit from years of sowing the gospel, it was a grieving process to walk away. I was fearful that I was leaving just because it was hard, and I didn't see that as a good reason to leave.

Wrestling before God with this decision, I distinctly remember a moment of prayer in the park near my home. I felt that God was releasing me from my role there. I felt that He was speaking to my heart that it is not failure when it is His hand that moves us on. I also sensed He was assuring me of His care for those I was discipling.

I was reluctant to tell the Mission Pastor at my sending church, believing he would think I was reneging on their ministry investment and wouldn't understand the new direction God was putting on my heart. I remember the relief that I felt after speaking with him, when he assured me that they would continue to support me through this transition and pray with me for God's direction. Again, when meeting with the missionary care people in my sending church I was afraid I would hear condemnation for leaving only five years after entering that culture. Instead, they listened as I shared what God had put on my heart and offered prayer and encouragement.

Journeying with Him

1. What are ways you can identify with this man's struggle to leave his ministry?
2. This missionary was able to deal with his anxiety over leaving uncompleted work behind as well as act on the desire to go in a new direction. What in his spiritual life and church relationships enabled him to do this? What might have happened in his next assignment had he not been able to make a healthy transition?
3. Questions that some church members and pastoral staff may have in a situation such as this are: If the missionary received a call to a particular country, people group and ministry, why would that call change? Did God want to change the missionary's direction or was he mistaken about where God was leading? Weren't they financed and trained for this particular work? Are those years learning the language and culture going to be wasted? How would you answer these questions if they came up in your church?
4. How would your church have responded to this missionary's desire to change ministries and countries? How would you like your church to care for a missionary in this kind of transition?

• • •

Consider the stress on children during a transition and how a disruption of schooling and separation of friendships will impact them. They will need to learn at a much earlier age how to say goodbye and grieve the loss of good friends. "Children can feel the pain, and they do not need to wait until they grow up to reflect on the experience and do something about the wounds." (O'Donnell, 2002, p. 65). *Third Culture Kids* (Pollock and Van Reken, 2009) is an excellent resource for parents and church caregivers who want to understand and help the children going through these transitions with their parents. Strengthening the missionary family is of primary importance for caregivers, because for many TCKs, home is where the family is (O'Donnell, 2002, p. 66).

Comfort the Children

One missionary veteran told me that my most important job overseas would be to comfort my children. I saw how vital this was when we moved to our new remote location. There was no English education available and the public schools were rough on foreigners. Our family came to a crisis point when one of our children had enough and wanted to go back to the states, yet the other wanted to stay. A counselor at our church helped us think through the issues and suggested an alternative that worked well for both the children as well as for our ministry overseas.

We were glad at the time for the blessing from our mission and supporting churches to move to the new, more remote location. Looking back, however, we wished someone had helped us consider the potential effect this transition might have on our children and helped us think through more options for our children's education.

Journeying with Them

1. When a family desires to make a move in their overseas ministry, we need to be affirming and supportive, but also ask the hard questions of how the children will fare in the new situation. What questions would be helpful to ask regarding the children?
2. It is easy to assume that agencies will consider the effect of a new move on the missionaries' children. After all, they are the entity most acquainted with the field and its resources for children, or lack thereof. How can a church care team collaborate with the agencies to make sure children's needs are not overlooked in these transitions?

• • •

Forced Out and Burned Out

My transition back to the U.S. was a difficult one. Due to visa problems, I had been forced out of my host country and was personally on the edge of burnout. Before I even left our field location, I contacted our home church for support and found a pastor who would meet with me regularly. I was coming home for a sabbatical and wanted to find someone to walk beside me on this road. His listening ear was a breath of fresh air. Besides him and his wife, my sabbatical team included other good friends and former missionaries. Our pastor was also very helpful in releasing church funds to secure needed counseling for burnout. A member of our church's care team opened their home for extended stays. A small fellowship group became a warm place of relational acceptance. The church was a great support at one of my lowest times.

When I transitioned back to the field, the church was also there for me. I was encouraged when they gave me a reception and opportunity to share the new vision. A counselor on our church's care team taught me a communication tool that would empower me in my new assignment and build strong relationships with my team. Someone else on the care team was assigned to track with me and occasionally debriefed my experience on the field. The emotional love I received was essential to sustaining me through this difficult transition.

Journeying with Her

1. Some Christians view the experience of burnout among Christian workers as a result of some emotional or spiritual deficiency. If caregivers had this view, how would that affect their attitude toward the worker? What are some other ways to view burnout?
2. What relationship factors were probably already present for this missionary, enabling her honesty about the burnout and openness to help? How do you cultivate relationships in your church for "such a time as this" in a missionary's life?
3. What was essential in this woman's recovery from burnout and transition back to the field? In what specific ways would your church be able to help so that burnout doesn't turn into one more missionary leaving the field?

• • •

Church Ambivalence

One huge issue we faced when leaving our host country was whether or not we would receive acceptance from the body of Christ in the midst of what we perceived as a failure. We had laid out the vision and told everyone how committed we were, then found that we could not perform as desired. I remember folks at church wanted us to come and see them, but we just wanted to hide.

One of the pastors who came and visited us had experienced a similar failure and wanted to reassure us. He said that what we'd learned had really taken us to a different level in understanding God's grace. We were so blessed by his visit. Likewise, some members of the church were part of an important committee who gave us guidance as we transitioned. That was marvelous. This really helped us to make the transition and feel confident that God was directing us.

However, there were other leaders in the church who weren't so easy to communicate with. At times we weren't sure they were behind us trying to find God's will to guide us. Reassurance from the leadership as to whether we were doing good work, or expectations regarding how we might improve our ministry would have been welcomed.

Journeying with Them

1. What are the key attitudes which scripture teaches us to have as we minister to Christian workers who have seemingly failed?
2. How can you encourage them to trust God and move forward with what He wants them to do?
3. How can a church avoid the contradictory messages from leadership that might confuse missionaries making main life transitions?

• • •

Going ... But Not Knowing

We completed our work in our host country and were spending a year at our home church before going to our new (as yet unknown) country and ministry. There were many questions that we were trusting God to answer. Where will our children be educated, and how will they do in the transition to the U.S.? Where will we stay and how will we get around? How will our church react to our not knowing where we were going next?

Our church was a dream come true. They were in touch with us months in advance to find out what our plans and needs were for the time we would be back. We stayed in a furnished condo that was donated to the church for missionaries' use. They loaned us a vehicle and even a cell phone. Church friends helped us find soccer tryouts, borrow a guitar and even find a Christian school that offered full scholarships to TCKs. One pastor helped us put together a video of our work. Doctors and dentists from our church provided free or substantially discounted care, including eye glasses. We have seen God's hand as he used the body of Christ to meet our needs.

On an emotional and spiritual level, many people from the church reached out to us and made us feel welcome. We all felt embraced by the various small groups available for fellowship and Bible study. The Pastor, as well as other church members, had us over for dinner either to hear about our experiences or just to spend time with us. The missionary care team and others in the mission department met with us, to ask questions about our experience and to listen to what was on our hearts about our children, our parents, our marriage, our walk with the Lord, and our future. We did not feel threatened at all but rather understood and accepted. The missionary prayer group welcomed us to share and prayed with us frequently. It was a joy to actively serve Christ in different church ministries alongside old and new friends in His body.

The hardest part was the uncertainty of not knowing for months what our next step would be. We wanted to continue serving the Lord overseas but didn't know where. Our missions department was especially sensitive, respectful and encouraging. We didn't feel pressure to make a quick decision as we trusted God together.

Journeying with Them

1. When moving overseas, some missionaries sell their car, house and most of their possessions. Imagine the faith it takes, knowing when they come back for an extended stay, they will bring only what they can carry in a few suitcases and rely on the good will of family, friends and church for the rest. What response should we have to that kind of faith and sacrifice?
2. How can your church welcome its missionaries so that their return is as seamless as possible?
3. How would you encourage their faith in God as they walk through "the uncertainty of not yet knowing" their next assignment?

CONCLUSION

One of our missionaries found two basic truths that guided his family when he studied about how people in the Bible successfully navigated through the changes they were facing. If you are following God, He promises to be with you and support you through the transitions. He expects you to fully trust and courageously obey Him even when you cannot see the end from the beginning (see Joshua 1:7-10).

Missionary life is a continuous string of transitions, some bigger than others. With a supportive body of believers back home, missionaries can be honest about their needs during the transition and keep on track with the mission God has given them. When the church steps up to fill these important gaps, Satan is defeated and those whom we send are empowered to build His worldwide church.

Chapter 15

Re-Entry, Retirement and Other Transitions

Bill & Betty Jane Born and David Wilson

> "And when Jesus had finished these parables, he went away from there, and coming to his hometown he taught them in their synagogue, so that they were astonished, and said, 'Where did this man get this wisdom and these mighty works? Is not this the carpenter's son? Is not his mother called Mary? And are not his brothers James and Joseph and Simon and Judas? And are not all his sisters with us? Where then did this man get all these things?' And they took offense at him. But Jesus said to them, 'A prophet is not without honor except in his hometown and in his own household.' And he did not do many mighty works there, because of their unbelief." (Matthew 13:53-58)

Jesus knows how to relate to returning missionaries. His experience recorded in the gospels as He returned home from serving on the 'mission field' provides a glimpse into His humanity. He is questioned, challenged and misunderstood by the people who knew Him well from His hometown. This is one of the few places in Jesus' ministry where He did not do miracles. He had great success in other places, but home was a challenge.

In this chapter, many of the reasons for returning home and how the church can help will be addressed. Transitions back to place of origin can be very difficult. In the missionary's mind, home may continue just like he left it. Transitions are even more difficult if the last term on the field was less than positive or productive. He may wonder what to share, or how much to divulge. He may question if the church will continue to support him or allow him to return to the field if he shares what really went on. Sometimes the return is temporary, and at other times it is permanent. The three broad categories of returns are Furlough/Home Assignment, Retirement, and Leaving the Ministry Permanently. Temporary departures include continuing education, additional training, aging parents, and insufficient financial support. A permanent departure may include returning to secular work, children leaving the field for advanced education, and premature returns due to moral failure, physical/psychological needs or a death in the family.

Regardless of the situation, there are many things a church can do to make a missionary's return encouraging, productive and beneficial to all concerned. This chapter will not describe these areas of transition, since there are numerous books and resources which thoroughly cover these topics. Instead, we will address the unique role which the church has to be a blessing and encouragement to its global workers in such transitions.

FURLOUGH (TEMPORARY HOME ASSIGNMENT)

The life of a missionary is full of major transitions. Their journey into this calling begins with leaving the comforts of home and country and learning to live a completely different life in unfamiliar surroundings. They learn to speak differently, eat differently, worship differently, and think differently. Even after their first term on the field, a temporary home visit can be challenging.

An Aisle for Cereal

A missionary family left for North Africa when their oldest child was four years old and their first term lasted four years. In order to acculturate to their host culture, the family only ate food served by the locals. For the last four years, their breakfast was either a warm chick-pea soup or a pasta dish with couscous. When they came home for a six month furlough, their church provided a gift card

> to a local grocery store, so they could go shopping upon arrival from the airport. As their now eight year old child walked through the aisles of the store, he had a stunned look on his face. There was an entire aisle dedicated to breakfast cereal. His mom and dad returned to the reality of the magnitude of choices in their home country and were overwhelmed. What was once a fairly simple and innocuous task of selecting a breakfast option had become a source of frustration.

This family experience is indicative of reverse culture-shock. They are beginning to realize that home is no longer 'home' as they knew it. At points along their journey, a separation takes place when the missionary family begins to adapt to the new way of life in their host culture. Even so, some missionaries have commented that they do not know where 'home' is anymore. Sometimes the closest thing to home is on the airplane between their host country and their place of origin.

There are many other symptoms of feeling like no place is home, covered very well by Neal Pirolo in his book *"The Reentry Team"* and in Marion Knell's book *"Burn up or Splash down: Surviving the Culture Shock of Reentry."* Many missionaries receive assistance from their sending agency when they return to their home culture. However, we have noticed that such help is often overlooked because of the other demands on the time of member care personnel. Therefore, a supporting church would do well to determine if there is a gap and seek to understand how to best come alongside their missionary.

The trauma over leaving the field of operation can be disorienting. Even for a temporary furlough, there may be some anxiety about leaving one's hard work in the hands of nationals for the next six to twelve months.

During the enculturation period, missionaries learn how to say goodbye like a local. In many places in the world, showing emotion is normal and expected, but if they are returning to a western culture, they may experience resistance to freely expressing emotion. Saying goodbye, even if temporary, never occurs without strong emotions. During the transition they may also experience other unrealistic expectations from people in their family, friends and home church.

Missionaries often begin to notice an abundance of materialism and excess in their home of origin that was overlooked before their departure for the field. They experience an incredibly challenging journey in their first term and their worldview has been greatly enlarged. Yet, their friends, family and even church is strangely unchanged. Some negative feelings are possible, like alienation, anger over materialism and complacency, judgmentalism and superiority over those who are not serving the Lord in difficult places. These feelings are subtle and rarely ever expressed externally, but if left unaddressed they may become a hindrance to a healthy home assignment.

Like every other human, missionaries have some delusions about the level of interest in their work which others may have. When someone has a career that takes them around the world, requires them to learn a different language, eat exotic foods, and experience God powerfully moving in exciting ways, there is the potential for overestimating the amount of interest others will have in hearing their stories. Frankly, if you are reading this book, you already have an interest in missionary stories. You are the proverbial "choir," to whom we are preaching. However, there are many people who just do not care about what happens in a little village among the Middle Atlas Mountains in North Africa. Unfortunately, for some missionaries, they return to friends, family, church members (and yes, even some pastors) who will only give them an obligatory amount of time to talk about their ministry.

Finally, a Time to Share What We've Been Doing

Frank and Sally completed their first term of service with an unreached people group. They were exhausted and ready for furlough. They could hardly wait to tell others what God had done in them and through them. They anticipated an evening talking with some of their closest friends about events of the past three years. They were especially eager to show items they had brought from the field and share their interesting stories. Dinner was ready when they arrived. Immediately they sat down to a good dinner prepared especially with food their hosts knew was unavailable overseas. It was a great meal. After dinner they took out their

> displays and began to talk. Five minutes later the phone rang. The hostess disappeared for about eight minutes. When she returned they moved on to the second show-and-tell item when the bottom dropped out. The host said, "Hey, let's take a break. I want to show you something." The host showed them his new boat purchased last summer. He was very excited to show them. One thing led to another and it was time to leave. In the car they commented to each other that they probably only spent 12 to 15 minutes sharing about what they did on the field. They were somewhat distressed, confused and disappointed.

With this foundation of insight, let's look at some ways we, as a church, can help prepare our returning missionaries to share their story while on home assignment:

1 — What to Share

Stories are always the most effective tool for communicating a ministry. In the western church, we are mostly task-oriented and frequently obsessed with project management. Most of the rest of the world is less task-oriented and more relationally-oriented. Oddly, those of us in the west are frequently refreshed by a good and compelling story. There is one word that will illustrate this point, "Hollywood." This is the place of the multi-billion dollar industry that does nothing more than tell stories. People go to experience these stories for their leisure time and spend large sums for that privilege. The movie industry is powerful, and it expends much time and energy to make its stories compelling and noteworthy.

Missionaries have some of the greatest stories to tell, yet they rarely take the time to make them compelling and noteworthy. We have the technology to enhance the stories and make them exciting, but what may happen is the missionary tries to share too much. Encourage your missionary to limit what they share. This may sound counter-productive, but there is a saying, "sometimes less is more."

For example, if the church has been supporting a missionary and contributing to a project fund, they will obviously need to give a report on the project. However, there are ways to make the project report more interesting.

Scenario 1 — Project/Task Oriented report:
"Last year, you gave $50,000 to help build a church in the village where we work. Here is a picture of the foundation being poured. Here is a picture of the bricks being made. Here is a picture of the walls being built. And here is the roof. Our first church service, 150 people attended and 13 people gave their lives to the Lord. We also have so many children that we are in need of a children's playground. Will you consider helping us with this project this year?"

Scenario 2 — Relationship Oriented report:
"Last year, you gave $50,000 to the people in the El Refugio village to help them build their church. As a result of this gift, we began church services with 150 people on the first day. This photo shows how full the church was that day. One of the children who came that day is Almondo. He was obviously from a poor family, but on this day he was dressed in his best shirt and pants. Almondo was very respectful and observant as he sat on the front row listening to every word from the pastor. When the time came at the end of the service for people to give their lives to the Lord, he was the first to raise his hand and spoke to the pastor afterwards. The next week, Almondo brought three of his friends from the community and they all sat on the front row and were very interested in all that the church was doing. Here is a picture of Almondo with his family and friends last Sunday just after he was baptised in the new baptismal. Because of his friendships in the community, we have so many children that we need to build a playground next to the church."

People send people to reach people. If all we wanted out of our missionaries was to build buildings, then there are more efficient and effective ways of doing that. Churches want to hear how their investment in a missionary is impacting the lives of people.

There are many other stories that could be told from this church, but the missionary chose to keep it down to only one. He chose Almondo's story because he had a purpose for sharing the need for a children's playground. Other stories would be just as compelling, but it is best to keep the number of stories to a minimum for maximum impact. One of the rules for storytelling is to "always keep them wanting to hear more." People will naturally want to hear more about this story as well as to hear others, so they are more likely to invite the missionary out for coffee or lunch and even to visit their small group or Sunday School class in church. Conversely, the opposite is true. If a missionary is sharing too much, then people are much more likely to avoid future contact.

The following basic elements of a story should be used every time a story is shared: an introduction, a climax, a conclusion, and then a moral to the story. This formula exists as a model for any well-told story. The lesson learned, or moral of the story, is especially important for a missionary to use.

One of the most important things a missionary can do when connecting with others, especially youth, is to confess a fault. Too often, church leaders will place missionaries on a pedestal and hold them in such high esteem that young people will conclude that they could never be good enough to serve God on the mission field. If a missionary includes a story of a 'lesson learned', then a bridge can be built for potential openness to a missionary calling. Also, the missionary should be vulnerable and share about negative experiences. However, the story should not end there, but leave room to accentuate the positive. For example, if the missionary lives in a place with no running water or electricity, it can leave a negative impression in the minds of kids. However, for those kids who like camping and the outdoors, rugged living might sound exciting. The story can then include how the Lord provided someone in the village who delivered water to their home every day and they shared the gospel with that person as a result of this relationship.

2 — How to Share

Technology can either be an aid to a presentation or a stumbling block for missionaries. If they are out of the country for many years, the technology they departed with has long been outdated. The care team may suggest that the missionary spend some time with someone well-versed in present-day media. The use of slide shows, audio, video and photos can either enhance a presentation or distract from it.

Missionaries are often mocked when they dress in native wear for their presentations and are sometimes seen as "out-of-touch." A good missionary care team will spend time with the missionary upon arrival and share current events from the church. This is a good time to help them prepare for their presentation and report to the congregation. Local churches are constantly changing and evolving into something new and different from year to year. Missionaries welcome relevant updates from people whom they know and trust.

Most people will tell you what you want to hear, but a true friend will tell you what you need to know. Being a true friend to missionaries sometimes means telling them something uncomfortable. Telling someone who just spent the last ten years working with people in a remote region of Southeast Asia that their clothing is not good enough for their Sunday night presentation may be a little harsh. Perhaps someone can take them shopping the day before their event for an outfit that will convey professionalism and relevance to the audience. This can also be especially helpful for teenagers, as they seek to 'fit-in' with their peers at church and potentially at school.

Endless slide shows of pictures can be boring. A true friend of the missionary may want to help them narrow down the number of photos and choose the ones which have the most impact. Volunteering to assemble the photos into a video with music may be even better. And for that matter, volunteering to listen to their story and help them tweak it to make it more interesting may be the most effective thing anybody can do for the missionary and for the church.

3 — Ways to Share

A missionary care team concerned about the success of their

missionaries on home assignment will help prepare them for speaking engagements. When helping a missionary prepare for a presentation, provide them with feedback that will encourage them to be brief, concise and specific in the stories they tell. Remember, always leave the audience wanting more. Hopefully, this will help them build bridges to the congregation as a whole and not just speak to those who are already committed to missions.

At Trinity Church, the Mission Pastor meets with the missionary immediately upon arrival. He typically does an interview where they share their stories. Each church is different, so each should design a route for missionaries to take once they arrive in country. We have a checklist and it follows this route:

1. Meet with the Mission Pastor and his wife
2. Meet with the Missionary Care Team
3. Meet with the Senior Pastor and his wife
4. Meet with the adopted small group during the week
5. Share a brief report with the congregation (5-7 minutes on Sunday morning)
6. Share in depth at a reception following Sunday morning services

These items are on the calendar before the missionary arrives. Apart from these six items, the missionary begins to network and set up their own meetings and events. There are some very creative ways to share. Cook native food and invite people to a meal featuring music, decorations and items from their host country. You may want to encourage your missionary to bring small gifts to give out as a thank you. Coins, stamps and other items do not cost much in other countries, but they have an enormous emotional 'currency' here at home. People will remember the gift and will be more likely to pray and support the missionary.

One of your roles as a care team while they are on home assignment is to help them connect with the church. If you set them up for success when they arrive, they are more likely to develop deeper and healthier relationships with people who may then become supporters when they return to the field.

MISSIONARY KID TRANSITION AFTER GRADUATION

As transitions from the field are discussed, the important adjustment high school seniors make in moving to their parents home culture is often overlooked after spending a lifetime overseas. "How TCKs [Third Culture Kids] do or don't do with the reentry experience can shape their lives for years to come... Normalizing this part of the TCK experience is as important as it is for so many other facets." (Pollock & Van Reken 2001, p 231). Whether the move is made alone or with the family, our church offers to help our students with registration and tuition costs to a two-week re-entry seminar with peers making similar transitions. Our desire is to help with their successful enculturation to North America as adults. We want them to thrive, not just to survive. The church invests the funds and the student invests two weeks of their first summer in the states. There are several seminars across the country. We are most familiar with and recommend the following:

- Barnabas International — on the west coast and in Ohio
- Interaction International — in Colorado
- Missionary Resources Connection — in South Carolina
- Some Christian colleges have their own re-entry seminars

Websites for current seminars are updated and made available on our website (MindTheGaps.org). The seminars are usually held in July or August each summer and registration is best secured in the fall before high school graduation to assure your student's placement. May you and your teen MKs be encouraged to look into the experienced assistance available from one of these programs as the transition approaches.

Thankful Teen

Thank you so much for sending me to the re-entry seminar. It has really helped me sort through some issues which I had thought I alone was having. Instead, I've found I am one of many. The program has helped me prepare for living in the States, something I hadn't ever imagined I'd need to do. Gratefully, (An MK from South America)

LEAVING THE FIELD PERMANENTLY

Ministry is very different than a secular job. Moving from one place to another for work may be exciting, but with missionaries there may not be the same level of excitement when leaving their adopted country and people. There may also be a significant change in the fulfillment and meaning he personally received from his ministry. The family will likely be leaving a place full of meaningful relationships with those who have become Christ-followers. They have become brothers and sisters in Christ instead of just colleagues in the workplace. They are often people with whom they prayed and have grown to love deeply. They have become a part of a family with a loving heavenly Father.

Throughout my lifetime, I (Bill) have lived in over a dozen places. Each place became home. However, "home" cannot be a geographical place or location only. There must be more to home than just coordinates. Here is a description of home from Ron & Bonnie Koteskey in their book, *Coming Home*:

> Remember that "home" is not so much a "place" as it is a situation in which you are known and trusted, understood and accepted, have predictable rituals and routine interactions with people among whom you feel secure, relaxed, and free to be yourself. If things have changed in your passport country, it will no longer feel like "home."
>
> - You may see many familiar faces, but few familiar people. They have changed.

- You may see familiar places, but they have been renovated and have new functions. They have changed.
- You may try familiar routines, but discover that you do not even know how to complete a purchase.

Nothing may come naturally anymore so that you feel like an alien in your own country. Feeling out of place back home may be much more alarming than when you felt out of place in a foreign country at the beginning of your term of service. You have become temporarily homeless, a marginal person functioning at the fringes of society, not at its core. The good news is that just as you became a part of your host culture, you can once again become a part of your passport culture if you wish to do so. As you write the next chapter of your life you can again feel like you are at home.

The missionary care team can help returning workers sort through their feeling of homelessness by debriefing and providing them with resources such as the book *Coming Home* (Koteskey, 2003). There are two very important questions regarding a permanent departure from the field:

- What is the *real* reason for the departure and the future?
- What is next?

Leaving the field permanently may include returning to take a position in the home office, going into secular work, leaving the field for children's educational needs, exiting due to moral failure, death in the family, health issues, possible further education or additional training, insufficient financial support to continue, helping aging parents, and many others.

The departing missionary family will definitely need a church body and team of caring individuals to walk alongside them during some difficult phases of the transition. They need people who will genuinely care and who will be good listeners. These need to be creative individuals, perceptive to the spiritual, emotional, physical and material needs change has created.

1 — Discover the needs

To better understand the needs of a returning missionary, one must look at the changes. Think through what has changed since the missionary departed his passport country. Of course the length of the list will be longer depending on the length of time since the original departure. Change may be found in both family and friends at home as well as in the returning missionary. Here is a quick list for consideration:

- Social (acceptability of new values)
- Financial (how money is spent, used or viewed as wasted)
- Emotional (sorrow, artificiality, hurting friends and family)
- Spiritual (many missionaries return home tired and spiritually dry)
- Physical (illness or injury)
- Family (births, deaths, marriage, divorce, empty nest, etc.)
- World-view (greater or limited)
- Sexual mores (change in what is socially "approved" or not)
- Technological (continuous, rapid changes)
- Entertainment (accepted, tolerated)
- Addictive behaviors (alcohol and drug use and other excesses)

Even though the material and physical needs are the most easily observed, they must not overshadow the importance of adjusting to this list of needs. Likewise the visible needs ought not to be neglected. If the sending agency has asked them to come home to take a needed place in the mission headquarters, it is quite possible the organization will be most helpful in assisting them in their new position and location. Of utmost importance for the care team is an awareness of the love and care that they can provide above and beyond what the agency offers. However, if they will no longer be serving with the sending agency, the responsibility will fall to family, friends and the church to assist in significant ways. There will be needs regardless of the reason they are returning home. They will vary according to their specific circumstances.

2 — Determine how to meet their needs

When returning from the field permanently, most of the same needs are present as in a temporary furlough, but they are often increased and even amplified. More time and energy may be required from the caregivers on your team and in your church. The gaps may be large, demanding more time and assistance. This is a great time to be prayerful, asking the heavenly Father for wisdom to perceive the visible and invisible needs of His children. When a care team is sensitive to the Spirit and faithful to His call, they are empowered to take action and meet the needs.

RETIREMENT

The word "retirement" is so sadly misunderstood. Many in the church view retirement as our culture does: "When I'm 65 I am going to: Quit work... Sit in a chair and take it easy... Relax... Buy a big screen TV and surround sound for my enjoyment... Spend the money I accumulated over the past 40 or 50 years... Play golf everyday..." Rarely do missionaries have a western cultural perspective on retirement. However, they will eventually arrive at a place where they move into this new season of life. This may include many goodbyes to national friends and life-long colleagues. This transition into this new season should, however, be well planned. That planning will require some different kinds of help and loving guidance. The church has the wonderful opportunity to come alongside of them.

There are some significant differences with a missionary's retirement. Missionaries resolutely chose to live with a different purpose and in a different environment, telling others the good news of Christ. They probably did not have incomes that provided for a summer home, large savings account and the accumulation of this world's "stuff." However, in recent years, mission sending agencies and supporting churches have been providing better retirement planning for the missionary to help them be ready for changes in the future.

One of the most important ways that the church can bless its missionaries is to require them to establish and contribute to a retirement fund. There are many ways to look at retirement from the perspective of a missionary. Some believe that the Lord will provide, so there is no need to plan ahead and save for retirement. Others believe in wise and careful planning for the future and follow the teachings of stewardship found throughout the book of Proverbs. The problem with the first group of missionaries is that they will eventually show up at the church in need of housing, food, transportation and all sorts of needs since they did not save for the future. Therefore, a wise missionary care team will take active steps to make sure all of their missionaries are preparing for their future retirement.

The church can also be a great help once the missionary returns to his home church to engage him in continuing his service to the Lord. Retirement can produce grief due to the loss of a lifetime of relationships. Be sensitive to those needs and watch for areas where the newly retired missionary can use his gifts, skills and vast global experience for the benefit of those in the church. How they serve within your church body will be somewhat dependent on their physical abilities combined with the particular skills they bring. Churches can greatly benefit by using the precious resource of these special servants within the congregation as leaders, strategists, consultants and a variety of other services to the local church. Perhaps they can serve on the missionary care team.

DEATH

While inevitable, we rarely plan for the death of one of our missionaries or of his family members. Yet, on occasion the unfortunate event comes either anticipated through prolonged illness, or suddenly by accident or attack. Almost always, a burial occurs rather quickly overseas, often within 24 hours. What should a church consider at such times? It needs to be as supportive as possible to the bereft family members. A natural place to begin is to consider what you would appreciate at such a time. You will naturally be limited by distance, should your missionary pass away on the field. Your first contact should simply include condolences and offer of help from a distance. A field visit is imperative as soon as possible. Send a member of the care team and/or a pastor to the field for counseling and grief support. Back home, you may want to provide a memorial service. What is important is that you demonstrate some visible and tangible expression of your love and care.

Above all, allow them time for planning what they will do next without pressure on a spouse to make quick decisions about the future. A hasty move is not expected of those in the congregation and should not be expected of your missionary. Graciously allow time for a widow or widower to make major decisions—six months to a year as they walk through the grief cycle. Contact the sending agency to learn what they have discussed. There are so many practical needs, for instance: counsel to develop a realistic budget, wise financial planning, appropriate insurance or other necessities. Often someone from your church or community could assist, helping avoid unfortunate mistakes at such a vulnerable time in their life.

Church's Oversight

A widow chose to remain in ministry overseas allowing her children to finish high school. However, her sending church abruptly dropped support. Because her husband had been a church planter, a ministry she could not continue on her own, the church no longer considered her in ministry. She ran a large guest house for traveling missionaries, becoming a liaison for language students in the country for the first time—ministries which she was well-qualified to fill. Her agency had a good relationship with the church, so they initiated contact explaining the importance of her new role. The church listened and after consideration deemed her as head-of-household and renewed her support allowing her to continue in the new role.

When it is necessary for a family to relocate to the States, help with as many details as necessary, especially if they move back to the church community. Our hope is the church and the missionary will be mutually blessed by the care given and received during such deep loss.

CONCLUSION

There are limitless transitions for missionaries to go through, but the important thing for churches to consider is to be intentional about caring for missionaries in the midst of the transition. Care for them as if they were members of your own family, because they are. Pray and ask for the Lord's wisdom and insight. Be sensitive to His leading and faithful to His call. Transitions are normal and they are often frustrating. Be prepared to love your missionary and to care for them deeply.

GET ON BOARD

1. Discuss the steps your missionaries are taking regarding future planning and retirement. What are the agency's retirement policies? Mind any gaps that you may find.

2. To better understand the stages of transition, read some of the literature on re-entry mentioned on our website, MindTheGaps.org.

3. Be certain your missionary is acquainted with church staff, mission committee members and the missionary care team.

4. When a missionary is on home assignment, have someone take them shopping to update their wardrobe.

5. Consider how your church could help MK graduates attend a re-entry seminar.

6. Determine what gaps need filling as your missionary family returns permanently, including the less obvious personal and emotional turmoil that may arise.

7. If appropriate, plan a celebration to honor the missionary leaving the field permanently, or plan a memorial service to pay tribute after a death.

Conclusion

THE MISSIONARY CARE TEAM AT TRINITY CHURCH

Several years have passed since we began this journey to care for our church's precious global workers and their families. The experience has been exhilarating at times, especially when we visit them overseas, get to know their resilient, multi-cultural children, and meet those who were influenced for Christ through them. At other times, our journey with them has taken us through the dark tunnels of their lives, their self-doubt in the midst of stress, their burnout or family difficulties. We are privileged to be with them through it all, to witness their hardiness and to be a part of seeing God's faithfulness in their lives.

In the introduction, we mentioned that this book is a record of "our journey thus far." To conclude, we'll recap some major themes which will serve as guides to keep you on track as you care for your church's missionaries.

- **Importance of Relationships** — The work of missionary care is a relational ministry. Relationships take time to build, but it is well worth the time and effort. Not only is it enjoyable to know missionaries, but developing deep relationships with them seems to be a vehicle through which God chooses to work in the world. Weave relationship building throughout your care for your missionaries. Your ministry to them, as well as their impact on your own life, will be powerful.

- **Intentionality of Care** — Missionary care was happening in our church in many wonderful ways before the establishment of the care team as is possibly the case in your church. The care team made missionary care much more intentional. Our team became a hub that served to guide the wheel of proactive care. Pray about how

God wants you to care for your missionaries so that they stay healthy and strong for His work. What are the core values that will guide everything you do, and what ways is your church uniquely equipped to identify and meet their needs? Don't wait for a crisis before you become involved.

- **Involvement of Entire Congregation** — Allow your care team to link with the wider family of God so that the whole church can experience the blessing of caring for missionaries. Think of the many ways God can use the manpower and resources within your church which He has so abundantly provided. As you widen the circle of care from your team to many others, missions will become infectious and missionaries will feel encouraged and supported.

- **Collaboration with mission agencies** — Give agencies their rightful place in the forefront of care for your missionaries. But realize that the task is too great for the agencies alone. There will be gaps of care that the church is uniquely equipped to fill. Find the key people in the mission agencies which are serving your church's missionaries. Find out from them, and your missionaries, ways in which your care team can complement, rather than duplicate what they do. Be careful, however, not to choose agencies whose lack of care produces a gap that is more than your church can handle.

- **Engagement of Resources** — Missionaries deserve the very best of care, and you will need support as you journey with them. This book is a good start, but there is much in the field that can inspire and instruct you. Take advantage of the bibliography and our website's helpful resources. Also, you won't regret the time or expense for the intensive training that can be gained in the variety of conferences on missionary care (see MindTheGaps.org).

We hope the journey you've taken with us has opened up vistas into the lives of God's global workers. Most of all, we wanted you to see the unique role of the church to empower its missionaries through its intentional care of them so that they can accomplish the work to which God has called them. Many churches are willing to care for their missionaries, but just aren't sure how. We pray that this book will help give you the confidence to step out and turn your church's willingness into reality. So, go and Mind the Gaps, to the glory of God and the good of His Church.

Author Biographical Information

Primary Authors:

David J. Wilson
William G. Britt, Ph.D.
Linda Parker, MFT
Susanne Hood
William G. (Bill) Born
Elizabeth J. (Betty Jane) Born

Other Contributors:

Don Bell
Paula Lawrence
Joan Morrill
Donna Stark

David J. Wilson, DMin. has a Master of Divinity degree from New Orleans Baptist Theological Seminary and a Doctorate from Campbell University. He has been serving as a Mission Pastor in the local church since 1996.

William G. Britt III, Ph.D. has a Master of Arts and Doctor of Philosophy degree in Clinical Psychology from Rosemead School of Psychology, Biola University. He is Associate Professor of Psychiatry at Loma Linda University School of Medicine and Senior Psychologist Specialist-Neuropsychology at Patton State Hospital. He has been on the Missionary Care Team since its inception.

Linda Parker received her bachelor's degree in Psychology from Wheaton College and her Masters degree in Counseling from Georgia State University. She was in private practice for 30 years before moving to Asia to counsel overseas workers.

Susanne Hood has a BA in Education from Seattle Pacific University, and MA in Education from Azusa Pacific University, and has served with Mission Aviation Fellowship for 37 years.

William G. (Bill) Born has a BS in Pastoral Studies, an Associate Degree in Missionary Aviation from Moody Bible Institute and an MS in Christian Counseling from Cairn University. He served with Mission Aviation Fellowship for 42 years as a pilot/mechanic in Brazil as the Director of Safety, and developed the Volunteer Ministry and initiated MAF Member Care.

Elizabeth J. (Betty Jane) Born has a BS in Education from Wheaton College and MS in Christian Counseling from Cairn University. She invested her missionary career in Brazil and her last ten years before retirement with Member Care at Mission Aviation Fellowship headquarters with her husband Bill. They have three children and nine grandchildren.

Bibliography

Addington, T. J., *Leading From the Sandbox.* Colorado Springs: NavPress, 2010.

American Psychiatric Association: Diagnostic & Statistical Manual of Mental Disorders, Fifth Edition. Arlington, VA 2013.

Borthwick, Paul. *Western Christians in Global Mission: What's the Role of the North American Church.* InterVarsity Press, 2012.

Britt III, William G. "The Prediction of Missionary Success Overseas Using Pretraining Variables." Ph.D. diss., Biola University, 1980.

Britt, William G. "Pretraining variables in the prediction of missionary success overseas." *Journal of Psychology and Theology,* 11, no. 34 (1983): 203-211.

Britt, William G. "Pretraining variables in the prediction of missionary success overseas." In *Helping Missionaries Grow: Readings in Mental Health and Missions,* edited by Kelly O'Donnell, & Michelle O'Donnell. Pasadena: William Carey Library, 1988.

Carter, Greg. *Skills, Knowledge, Character: A Church-Based Approach to Missionary Candidate Preparation.* Valparaiso, Ind.: Turtle River Press, 2010.

Curran, Delores. *Traits of a Healthy Family.* Winston Press, 1983.

Dodds, Lois A. and Lawrence E. "Am I Still Me: Changing the Core Self to Fit a New Cultural Context." (Presented at the American Association of Christian Counselors World Congress, Dallas, TX. Nov. 6-8, 1997).

Eriksson, C. J. Bjorck and A. Abernethy. "Occupational Stress, Trauma and Adjustment in Expatriate Humanitarian Aid Workers," *Stress and Trauma Handbook: Strategies for Flourishing in*

Demanding Environments, edited by J. Fawcett, 68-100. Monrovia, CA: World Vision, 2003.

Foster, Richard J. *Celebration of Discipline: The Path to Spiritual Growth*. New York, NY: HarperCollins Publishers, 1998.

Foyle, Marjory F. *Overcoming Missionary Stress*. Wheaton, Ill: Evangelical Mission Information Service, 1989.

Hay, Rob. *Worth Keeping: Global Perspectives on Best Practice in Missionary Retention*. Pasadena, Calif: William Carey Library, 2007.

Hoke, Steve and Bill Taylor. *Global Mission Handbook: A Guide for Crosscultural Service*. Downers Grove, Ill: Intervarsity Press, 2009.

IFMA Missions, "*Dropouts-Burnouts-Forceouts-Never-should-have-Gone-outs" IFMA News and Trends* article Vol. 49:1, April 1998 (www.IFMAMissions.org, accessed 2014).

Jordan, Peter. *Re-Entry: Making the Transition from Missions to Life at Home*. Seattle, Wash.: YWAM Publishing, 1992.

Keller, Timothy. *Counterfeit Gods: The Empty Promises of Money, Sex, and Power, and the Only Hope that Matters*. New York, NY: Penguin Group Publishers, 2009.

Koteskey, Ron and Bonnie. *Coming Home: The Reentry Transition*. Wilmore, KY: New Hope International Ministries, 2003.

http://www.missionarycare.com/ebooks/Reentry_Book_Kotesky.pdf (accessed February 18, 2014).

MacMillan, Pat, *The Performance Factor*, Nashville: Broadman and Holman Publishers, 2001.

McCulley, Carolyn. *Keeping the Peace in E-mail Communication, PeaceMaker.net, 2000.*

Miller, Sherod et. al. *Collaborative Marriage Skills*, Evergreen, Co: Interpersonal Communications Programs, Inc., 2007.

Newell, Marvin. "Excellence in Missions: Best Practices from Missio Nexus." *Evangelical Missions Quarterly*, January 2009.

O'Donnell, Kelly. *Doing Member Care Well: Perspectives and Practices from Around the World.* Pasadena: William Carey Library, 2002.

O'Donnell, Kelly. *Global Member Care, Volume One.* Pasadena: William Carey Library, 2011.

O'Donnell, Kelly and Michèle Lewis O'Donnell. *Global Member Care, Volume Two.* Pasadena: William Carey Library, 2013.

Parks, Helen Jean. *Holding the Ropes: Intercessory Prayer for Missions.* Nashville: Broadman Press. 1983.

Pirolo, Neal. *Serving as Senders.* San Diego: Emmaus Road International, 1991.

Pirolo, Neal. *Serving as Senders—Today.* San Diego: Emmaus Road International, 2012.

Pirolo, Neal. *The Reentry Team: Caring for your Returning Missionaries.* San Diego: Emmaus Road International, 2000.

Pollock, David C. and Ruth E.VanReken. *Third Culture Kids: Growing Up Among Worlds.* Boston: N. Brealey Publishers, 2001, Rev. 2009.

Prins, Marina and Braam Willemse. *Member Care for Missionaries: A Practical Guide for Senders.* South Africa: Member Care Southern Africa, 2009.

Reagon, Wilson and David Kronbach. *Tender Care.* Rockford, Ill: Barnabas International, 2010.

Sande, Ken. *The Peacemaker: A Biblical Guide to Resolving Personal Conflict.* Grand Rapids: Baker Books, 2004.

Schaefer, Frauke C., et al. "Traumatic events and posttraumatic stress in cross-cultural mission assignments." *Journal of Traumatic Stress* 20, no. 4, 2007.

Schaefer, Frauke C., and Charles A. Schaefer. *Trauma and Resilience: Effectively Supporting those who Serve God — A Handbook*. Condeo Press, 2012.

Schultz, Doris M. "Re-entry: An Introduction." *Enhancing Missionary Vitality*, edited by John R. Powell and Joyce M. Bowers, Minneapolis: Augsburg-Fortress Publishers, 1999.

Serving Together: A Handbook for Partnership. Orlando: Pioneers, 2012.

Swanson, Bruce. "Whirling Teacups: A Bi-Cycle Analysis of Missionary Growth." *Enhancing Missionary Vitality*, edited by John R. Powell and Joyce M. Bowers, Minneapolis, Augsburg-Fortress Publishers, 1999

Tuckman, Bruce, 1965. "Developmental Sequence in Small Groups," *Psychological Bulletin* 63, no. 91/4(6), 1965.

Van Scyoc, Mark. Embracing *World Changers: A Survival Guide for Missionaries and their Supporters.* Leola, Penn: Partnership Publications, 2006.

Williams, Kenneth. "Characteristics of the More Successful and Less Successful Missionaries". PhD. Diss. US International University, 1973.

Wilson, Reagon and David Kronbach. *Tender Care: Providing Pastoral Care for God's Global Servants.* Rockford, Ill: Barnabas Books, 2010.

Winter, Ralph, "The Two Structures of God's Redemptive Mission", Campus for Christ http://resources.campusforchrist.org/images/4/48/The_Parachurch.pdf

Wuest, Kenneth. *Word Studies in the Greek New Testament, Volume III.* Grand Rapids: Eerdmans Publishing Co., 1975.